D0777507

DISCOVERING GOD
IN STORIES FROM THE BIBLE

Crossway books by Philip Graham Ryken

Courage to Stand
Jeremiah's Battle Plan for Pagan Times

Discovering God in Stories from the Bible

The Heart of the Cross
with James Montgomery Boice

DISCOVERING
GOD

In Stories from the Bible

PHILIP GRAHAM RYKEN

FOREWORD BY
JAMES MONTGOMERY BOICE

CROSSWAY BOOKS • WHEATON, ILLINOIS
A DIVISION OF GOOD NEWS PUBLISHERS

Discovering God in Stories from the Bible

Copyright © 1999 by Philip Graham Ryken

Published by Crossway Books
a division of Good News Publishers
1300 Crescent Street
Wheaton, Illinois 60187

Cover photo: The Stock Market

Cover design: David LaPlaca

First printing, 1999

Printed in the United States of America

Library of Congress Cataloging-in-Publication Data
Ryken, Philip Graham, 1966-
   Discovering God in stories from the Bible / Philip Graham Ryken.
     p.   cm.
   Includes biographical references.
   ISBN 1-58134-113-X
   1. God—Attributes. 2. God—Attributes—Biblical teaching.
 I. Title.
BT130.R95 1999
231'.4—dc21   99-25599
                                            CIP

15	14	13	12	11	10	09	08	07	06	05	04	03	02	01	00	99
15	14	13	12	11	10	9	8	7	6	5	4	3	2	1		

To Dr. and Mrs. James and Elaine Maxwell—
Their lives are constant illustrations of divine love.

CONTENTS

FOREWORD

by
James Montgomery Boice

"Nearly all the wisdom we possess, that is to say, true and sound wisdom, consists of two parts: the knowledge of God and of ourselves." Those words from the opening paragraph of John Calvin's *Institutes of the Christian Religion* are as true today as when they were written more than four centuries ago. But the world has not grown wiser for them. On the contrary, people in our day, even in the church, know very little about God and therefore do not know themselves well either, if at all. For the most part people have turned away from God and have plunged even deeper into the sad spiritual ignorance of our times.

Philip Ryken, my esteemed colleague at Tenth Presbyterian Church in Philadelphia, has made a bold attempt at turning the tide of ignorance with this book. He is well aware that people do not like theology and that many will never pick up a book on God's attributes, let alone read it. But people do like stories. So in a winsome and creative manner, he has attempted to explore the character of God through thirteen Bible stories that have been given to teach us who God really is.

Should you read this book? Does getting to know God matter? Let me suggest four reasons why you should read it and why getting to know God is a vitally important matter.

First, it is by getting to know God that a person experiences what the Bible refers to as *eternal life*. Jesus indicated this when he prayed, "This is eternal life: that they may know you, the only true God, and Jesus Christ, whom you have sent" (John 17:3). To have eternal life means to be made alive to God so you can enjoy him now, live to the fullest extent, and know that you will continue to have fellowship with God in heaven when you die. It is what Jesus meant when he said, "I am the resurrection and the life. He who believes in me will live, even though he dies; and whoever lives and believes in me will never die" (John 11:25-26).

Second, knowledge of God means getting to *know ourselves,* as I said at the beginning. Our day is the day of the psychiatrist, psychologist, and counselor. People spend billions of dollars annually in an attempt to know themselves, to sort themselves out. But the deepest knowledge of ourselves does not come by counseling. To know ourselves, we must know that we have been created in the image of God himself, that we have fallen from that high position through sin, and that God has sent his Son, the Lord Jesus Christ, to rescue us from our sin that we might become again what he has intended us to be. That knowledge comes through God's self-revelation.

To gain that knowledge is a humbling experience, because none of us wants to face up to our sin naturally. It is painful too. Isaiah had a vision of God seated on his heavenly throne, and he cried out, "Woe to me! I am ruined! For I am a man of unclean lips, and I live among a people of unclean lips, and my eyes have seen the King, the LORD Almighty" (Isa. 6:5). And he was a prophet! At the same time, the discovery of who we are is both reassuring and satisfying. For instead of trying to be something we are not, we learn to be what God intended us to be. We learn that God does not love us because we are good but in spite of our being bad, and that he will remake us.

Third, knowledge of God gives us *knowledge of this world.* The world is merely the individuals who compose it written large, and these need to come to a knowledge of God too. Knowing God helps us know why things go so wrong in this world and what needs to be done about it. Telling others about God is also the most important thing we can do to help them.

Fourth, getting to know God leads to *personal holiness*, for God is holy, and those who know him will become increasingly like him. God has said, "Be holy, because I am holy" (Lev. 11:45). Most people do not worry about becoming holy very much. They hardly know what holiness means. But if the cause of our failures and miseries is sin, which the Bible says it is, then the way to true success and genuine joy is to become like God, which is what getting to know God will lead to.

This is the message of some of the most important verses in the Bible about getting to know God. The prophet Jeremiah wrote:

> *"Let not the wise man boast of his wisdom*
> *or the strong man boast of his strength*
> *or the rich man boast of his riches,*
> *but let him who boasts boast about this:*
> *that he understands and knows me,*
> *that I am the LORD, who exercises kindness,*
> *justice and righteousness on earth,*
> *for in these I delight,"*
> *declares the LORD.* (Jer. 9:23-24)

Like any book about God, *Discovering God* will only point you in the right direction. It will not believe for you or pray for you. You have to do those things for yourself. *Discovering God* will not even teach you all you ought to know about God. God is an infinite being, and no finite being will ever come to know God completely. But these thirteen bright chapters will get you started. And they will encourage you too. As you start to read, remember that God has promised that those who seek him will find him and that to those who knock, the door "will be opened" (Matt. 7:7-8).

PREFACE

I long to know God more intimately. At least, sometimes I do. The rest of the time I am too busy for God, oblivious to the greatness of his glory. But deep down, my heart's desire is to know and love the God who has always known and loved me.

The way to know God better is to study him. The way to study him is to learn what the Bible teaches about him, for all God's attributes are revealed in God's Word. Though difficult, the contemplation of God is the most rewarding of all endeavors. In the words of Charles Haddon Spurgeon:

> There is something exceedingly improving to the mind in a contemplation of the Divinity. It is a subject so vast, that all our thoughts are lost in its immensity; so deep, that our pride is drowned in its infinity. . . . Nothing will so enlarge the intellect, nothing so magnify the whole soul of man, as a devout, earnest, continuing investigation of the great subject of the Deity.[1]

Unfortunately, somewhere along the way the evangelical church lost Spurgeon's enthusiasm for investigating God. Contemporary Christians have an unworthy concept of deity. We are interested in too many other things. We want to be entertained rather than enlightened, distracted rather than discipled. To put it bluntly, God bores us.

If there is one thing that holds our attention, however, it is a good story. And, as everyone knows, the best stories of all are in the Bible. With this in mind, this book uses stories from the

Bible to teach the attributes of God. Each chapter includes doctrinal instruction on one aspect of God's character, but it also uses a Bible story to illustrate, explain, and apply it to daily life.

Studying the divine attributes in this or any other way is dangerous. The danger is to treat God like a specimen in a laboratory, academically rather than spiritually, knowing about him rather than actually knowing him. The German Reformer Philipp Melanchthon warned of this when he wrote, "We do better to adore the mysteries of deity than to investigate them. What is more, these matters cannot be probed without great danger, and even holy men have often experienced this."[2]

If the mysteries of God's character are to be adored, they must be investigated, of course, but Melanchthon was right to warn us. The right way to study God is to worship him for his attributes, so that our theology becomes our doxology.

Theology does not become doxology on its own. For this we need the help of God's Spirit. Melanchthon was discipled in the Christian faith by Martin Luther, who knew there was "a great difference between knowing *that* there is a God and knowing *who* he is and what he is like. Nature knows the first, and it is written in all our hearts. The second is taught only by the Holy Spirit."[3]

The Holy Spirit has been my helper as I have worked on this book (the errors are mine, not his!). But I have had many other helpers as well. As always, I am grateful for the love of my family, the prayers of my congregation, and the support of the staff at the Tenth Presbyterian Church in Philadelphia. The Reverend John Yenchko suggested ways to shape the outline, and a number of readers sharpened the text, chiefly Holly Canavan, Jonathan Rockey, Mary Ryken, and Glenn Wesley.

CHAPTER 1

TO GOD BE THE GLORY

The Story of Moses on God's Mountain

∽

Who is he, this King of glory?
The Lord Almighty—he is the King of glory.

PSALM 24:10

How much does God weigh?

If David Wells is right, God is not tipping the scales the way he used to. In a book called *God in the Wasteland*, Wells describes a curious condition he calls "the weightlessness of God." He writes:

> It is one of the defining marks of Our Time that God is now weightless. I do not mean by this that he is ethereal but rather that he has become unimportant. He rests upon the world so inconsequentially as not to be noticeable. He has lost his saliency for human life. Those who assure the pollsters of their belief in God's existence may nonetheless consider him less interesting than television, his commands less authoritative than their appetites for affluence and influence, his judgment no more awe-inspiring than the evening news, and his truth less compelling than the advertisers' sweet fog of flattery and lies. That is weightlessness.[1]

It is the weightlessness of God, more than anything else, that explains the failings of the evangelical church. It is because God is so unimportant to us that our worship is so irreverent, our fellowship so loveless, our witness so timid, and our theology so shallow. We have become children of a lightweight God.

HOW TO GAIN WEIGHT

One of the best ways for our knowledge of God to regain some weight is by contemplating his attributes. The proper place to begin is with God's glory, for that is what "glory" means: the weightiness of God.

The Hebrew word for "glory" (*kavod*) comes from the Hebrew word for "heavy" (*kaved*). The word was often used to describe things that were heavy in the literal, physical sense. The Bible says the high priest Eli was "heavy" (1 Sam. 4:18). In other words, he was fat.

The word was also used more figuratively to describe anything substantial or impressive. The Bible says Abraham was "heavy," but it had nothing to do with his waistline. It meant that he was wealthy. "Abram had become very wealthy [literally, "heavy"] in livestock and in silver and gold" (Gen. 13:2).

Eventually, the Hebrew word for "heavy" was used to describe anyone who deserved honor or recognition. It was used for warriors, princes, merchants, and other men of position and influence. In modern English, we would call them "heavyweights."

The biggest heavyweight of all is Almighty God (not physically, of course, but spiritually). No one is more substantial than he is. No one has more influence. No one has a higher position or a weightier reputation. No one is more deserving of honor, recognition, and praise. However weightless he may seem in the postmodern church, God himself is heavy. In other words, he is glorious.

What is the glory of God? God's glory is so far beyond our comprehension that it is hard to put into words. Perhaps this is why most books on the attributes of God leave glory off the list. It is not so much an attribute in itself as the sum of all God's attributes. Holiness, justice, goodness, power, truth—every one of the divine perfections adds to God's reputation, and hence to the weightiness of his glory.

God is glorious in what he *does*. He is glorious in creation. His divine attributes—his power and his wisdom—are revealed in everything he has made, from the smallest subatomic particle to the farthest galaxy.

The Creator God is so heavy that he has left his imprint on the universe like a work boot in wet cement. "The heavens declare the glory of God; the skies proclaim the work of his hands" (Ps. 19:1). In the same way that the skill of an artist is displayed in his artwork, the transcendence of God is displayed in his handiwork. "Be exalted, O God, above the heavens; let your glory be over all the earth" (Ps. 57:11). God is the glorious Creator.

God is also the glorious Redeemer. His glory is displayed in redemption as well as in creation. God brings glory to himself whenever he saves his people. This is the meaning of the Exodus. When the children of Israel were enslaved in the land of Egypt, God delivered them by mighty deeds of power. But first he explained to Moses why he was going to do it: "I will gain glory for myself through Pharaoh and all his army, and the Egyptians will know that I am the LORD" (Ex. 14:4). God enhances his reputation every time he saves his people. He is as glorious in redemption as he is in creation; he is glorious in everything he does.

God is also glorious in who he *is*. He is glorious in and of himself. Even if God had never made anything or saved anyone, he would still be glorious in his being. It is God's very nature to be heavy.

However, there would be no way for human beings to experience the glory of God's being unless somehow he revealed it. That is why God sometimes gives glimpses of his glory. The

Bible includes historical accounts of visible manifestations of God's weightiness.

On occasion God revealed himself in a cloud of dazzling, brilliant light. He led the people out of Egypt with a cloud by day and a pillar of fire by night. The Bible calls this radiant, luminescent cloud "the glory of the Lord" (Ex. 16:10).

This is the glory-cloud—sometimes called the "shekinah" glory—that the prophet Ezekiel saw at the temple. "The glory of the LORD rose from above the cherubim and moved to the threshold of the temple. The cloud filled the temple, and the court was full of the radiance of the glory of the LORD" (Ezek. 10:4). What Ezekiel saw was a visible manifestation of the invisible attributes of God. "Glory," wrote the Puritan Thomas Watson (d. 1686), "is the sparkling of the Deity."[2]

THE GLORY OF GOD IN THE FACE OF MOSES

There is a story in the Bible about the sparkling of God's deity. It is the story of Moses on God's mountain.

God had invited Moses up to Mount Sinai for the world's first summit meeting. He wanted to issue his policy statement on human behavior, sometimes called the Ten Commandments. But when Moses went back down the mountain and started telling people what to do, how would they know that he wasn't just making it up as he went along? They needed some evidence that God was actually speaking to Moses.

In order to give the people a visible manifestation of his weightiness, God descended on the mountain in the bright cloud of his glory.

> *When Moses went up on the mountain, the cloud covered it, and the glory of the LORD settled on Mount Sinai. For six days the cloud covered the mountain, and on the seventh day the LORD called to Moses from within the cloud. To the Israelites the glory of the LORD looked like a consuming fire*

on top of the mountain. Then Moses entered the cloud as he
went on up the mountain. And he stayed on the mountain
forty days and forty nights. (Ex. 24:15-18)

The glory of God burned like fire on the mountain. It was so incandescent that it filled the people with fear. They said, "This great fire will consume us, and we will die if we hear the voice of the LORD our God any longer" (Deut. 5:25). That gives a fairly good indication how heavy God is. Whenever mortal beings have felt even the slightest weight of his glory, they have seriously doubted whether they would live to tell about it.

Moses did live to tell about it, even though he made the most audacious (not to say foolhardy) demand anyone has ever made of God. Once he had received some assurance that God was going to stay with his people, he said, "Now show me your glory" (Ex. 33:18).

There is one sense in which Moses had already seen the glory of God. He had seen the pillar of cloud by day and the pillar of fire by night. He had been surrounded by the glory-cloud when the Lord descended upon the mountain. But Moses wanted more. He wanted to experience God more directly. He wanted to know God more intimately. He wanted to be wrapped up in the glory of God.

Moses had no idea what he was really asking. What he was asking was impossible, as God told him: "You cannot see my face, for no one may see me and live" (Ex. 33:20). In other words, it is impossible to see the invisible God as he is in himself. For mortal beings, there is something overwhelming, even destructive, about the weight of God's glory.

God was gracious *not* to show Moses his glory, but there was one thing he said he would do. "Then the LORD said, 'There is a place near me where you may stand on a rock. When my glory passes by, I will put you in a cleft in the rock and cover you with my hand until I have passed by. Then I will remove my hand and you will see my back; but my face must not be seen'" (Ex. 33:21-23).

That is what Moses saw, what God called the "back" of his glory. And that is *all* he saw. Yet there is more glory in God's back than there is in the whole universe. Even the reverse side of his majesty was glorious beyond anything any human being had ever seen before. That is why Moses was so luminous when he went back down God's mountain. "When Moses came down from Mount Sinai with the two tablets of the Testimony in his hands, he was not aware that his face was radiant because he had spoken with the LORD" (Ex. 34:29).

The glory of God was reflected in the face of Moses. This was the afterglow of his mountaintop experience. Some of the radiant resplendence of Almighty God was still shining in his countenance.

The people took one look at Moses, and they were afraid. Even when it is only reflected in the face of a human being, the glory of God demands fear and worship. "When Aaron and all the Israelites saw Moses, his face was radiant, and they were afraid to come near him" (Ex. 34:30).

The face of Moses teaches two things about God's glory. First, it shows that human beings are capable of reflecting the glory of God. Only God is all-glorious in himself, yet we are made to reflect the light of his glory. What Moses looked like when he came down from God's mountain is what human beings were *supposed* to look like all along. God made us a little lower than the heavenly beings, crowned with glory and honor (Ps. 8:5). This is not merely a figure of speech. Since we are made in God's image, we are capable of shining with God's glory, as Moses was.

Second, the face of Moses shows how glorious God must be by comparison. All Aaron saw was the reflection of the back of God's glory in his own brother's face. Yet what he saw was so glorious that he was afraid to look at it. It was too magnificent, too glorious, too heavy. Moses had to reassure his brother that everything was okay.

Once Moses had repeated the commands God had given him on the mountain, he covered his face. Afterwards, "whenever he entered the LORD's presence to speak with him, he removed the veil until he came out. And when he came out and told the Israelites what he had been commanded, they saw that his face was radiant. Then Moses would put the veil back over his face until he went in to speak with the LORD" (Ex. 34:34-35). The people had to be shielded from the brightness of God's glory. Even its reflection was too much for them to bear.

THE GLORY OF GOD IN THE FACE OF CHRIST

The apostle Paul once wrote about the glory of God in the face of Moses. He explained that "the Israelites could not look steadily at the face of Moses because of its glory" (2 Cor. 3:7).

Then Paul went on to describe something even more glorious, something he had seen with his own eyes. It was something so resplendent that, by comparison, the face of Moses lost all its luster. Paul had gazed upon the face of Jesus Christ (Acts 9:3-6). Once he had seen Jesus, he said that "what was glorious has no glory now in comparison with the surpassing glory" (2 Cor. 3:10). By "surpassing glory," he meant "the light of the knowledge of the glory of God in the face of Christ" (2 Cor. 4:6).

All the attributes of God are displayed in Jesus Christ. Jesus of Nazareth was a real man, but he was more than a man. He was God as well as man. Because of his divine nature, Jesus possesses every divine attribute, including God's glory, which is the cumulative weight of all the rest of his attributes. "The Son is the radiance of God's glory and the exact representation of his being" (Heb. 1:3a). The Son has the same infinite weight of being as the Father.

There are hints of Christ's glory all through the Gospels.

He was born in glory. True, he was born into an ordinary family in an ordinary place. But there was nothing ordinary about his birth announcement! When the angels appeared to the shepherds, "the glory of the Lord shone around them" (Luke 2:9), and they heard the angels say, "'Glory to God in the highest'" (v. 14a).

As the Christ child grew to manhood, the glory of his deity was concealed by his humanity. But every now and then a ray of his splendor would shine forth. Jesus revealed his glory, the Bible says, when he turned the water into wine (John 2:11). He brought glory to God the Father by raising Lazarus from the dead (John 11:4). When he came to the end of his life, he was able to say to his Father, "'I have brought you glory on earth by completing the work you gave me to do'" (John 17:4).

There was even one occasion when Christ's glory shone through in all its brilliance. It was when Peter, James, and John went up on God's mountain, like Moses before them. "There he [Jesus] was transfigured before them. His face shone like the sun, and his clothes became as white as the light" (Matt. 17:2). In fact, Moses was there, too, talking with Jesus (v. 3). Moses finally got to see what he had asked to see more than a thousand years before!

What Moses and the disciples saw was God's Son in all God's glory. Jesus was "switched on," as if he had gone from parking lights to high beams, so that the disciples could witness his eternal glory. They were shown a visible manifestation of the weight of his divine being.

Then Jesus died. There was nothing glorious about his death. The crucifixion was an ugly, bloody, messy business, an agony of thorns, splinters, and nails. Christ died a cursed death on the cross.

But what Christ accomplished through his death was glorious. In a way, it was the most glorious thing he did. He took God's punishment for our sin upon himself. Jesus did this in such a way that he retained exclusive rights to the glory of our salvation. He paid the entire debt of our sin on the cross. We cannot claim any credit for any part of our forgiveness. Jesus paid it all so that all the glory would belong to God. He offered the sacrifice. He made the atonement. Therefore, to him and to him alone belongs all the glory.

Once Jesus had suffered for sin, he "was taken up in glory" (1 Tim. 3:16). There he reigns, with his majestic glory illuminating the courts of heaven. There he is worshiped, for he alone is "worthy . . . to receive glory" (Rev. 4:11).

At the end of the ages, the glorious Christ will come again. Whenever the New Testament mentions his Second Coming, it emphasizes how glorious the event will be. Jesus promised he would return "'in his Father's glory with his angels'" (Matt. 16:27). He will come "'on the clouds of the sky, with power and great glory'" (Matt. 24:30b). "'When the Son of Man comes in his glory, and all the angels with him, he will sit on his throne in heavenly glory'" (Matt. 25:31). The same Christ who was raised in glory will reign in glory forever and ever.

GIVE HIM ALL THE GLORY

If God is so glorious, then we ought to give him all the glory we can. This is why God made us in the first place. He made us for his glory (Isa. 43:7).

"What is the chief end of man?" asks the first question of the Westminster Shorter Catechism. It is a question about the ultimate meaning of human existence. What is life all about? The answer is: "Man's chief end is to glorify God, and to enjoy him forever."

That is a good answer, maybe even the best answer, but it raises another question. If God is glorious in all he is and does, then how can we give any glory to him?

We cannot add any weight to God. He is already completely

glorious in himself. But what we can do is reflect his glory, the way Moses reflected it when he came down from God's mountain.

A person who glorifies God is like one of the mirrors in a powerful telescope. When an astronomer looks through his telescope, he is not trying to see the mirrors inside. Yet actually that is what he is looking at—not stars, but mirrors. By their reflection, those mirrors enable him to see the bright stars of the heavens. In the same way, the followers of Christ reflect the glory of God. We have no glory of our own. Whatever glory we have is a reflection of God's glory.

How can you reflect God's glory? First, by putting your faith in him. Until you trust God, it is doubtful whether you can glorify him at all. You have to begin by admitting that you cannot save yourself, that only Jesus can save you. Once you do that, then all the glory for your salvation will return to God. You will be like Abraham, who "was strong in faith, giving glory to God" (Rom. 4:20 KJV).

Next, glorify God by confessing your sins. There was a man in the Bible who glorified God by confessing his sin. His name was Achan. He committed a sin that involved deceit, treachery, theft, and in a way, murder. When Achan's sin was discovered, he was brought before Joshua, the leader of God's people.

What Joshua said to Achan is significant: "'My son, give glory to the LORD, the God of Israel, and give him the praise. Tell me what you have done; do not hide it from me'" (Josh. 7:19). Achan confessed his sin, and then he was taken out and executed for his crime. The Bible does not say whether he was granted eternal life or not. Perhaps he was. But in any case, Achan glorified God by confessing his sin. Repentance, as well as faith, gives glory to God.

Then glorify God in your worship. This is what the psalms so often call us to do. "Ascribe to the LORD the glory due his name" (Ps. 29:2a). "Sing the glory of his name; make his praise glorious!" (Ps. 66:2a). "I will praise you, O Lord my God, with all my heart; I will glorify your name forever" (Ps. 86:12). Whenever we worship God, we do what we were made to do. In our prayers and praises we declare that God alone is glorious.

How else can you glorify God? Glorify God by your good works. Jesus said, "'This is to my Father's glory, that you bear much fruit, showing yourselves to be my disciples'" (John 15:8). The fruit Jesus had in mind is the fruit of good works. So give God the glory by feeding the hungry, clothing the naked, healing the sick, loving the orphans, and helping everyone in need.

Glorify God by telling other people about Jesus every chance you get. If they are led to trust God and repent for their sins, then God will have gained another worshiper.

Glorify God by supporting the work of missions. The reason the church sends out missionaries is to "declare his glory among the nations, his marvelous deeds among all peoples" (1 Chron. 16:24). To pray for or pay for a missionary is to help spread God's glory.

Glorify God with your art and music, by what you make and what you perform. One man who did this was Johann Sebastian Bach, who signed his compositions "S. D. G.," which stands for *soli Deo gloria*, "to God alone be the glory." Another good example is the jazz musician Duke Ellington, who wrote *Concerts of Sacred Music*. Bach and Ellington wrote and played their music to the glory of God. Even if you are less talented than they are, you can give glory to the same God.

Glorify God in your play by resting in his goodness. Glorify him in your work by working with all your strength. Glorify him in the menial tasks of the home. God receives glory whenever a dish is washed, a floor is mopped, a newspaper is recycled, or even a diaper is changed in his name.

In short, glorify God in any and every activity of life by doing it in his service and according to his will. "So whether you eat or drink or whatever you do, do it all for the glory of God" (1 Cor. 10:31).

If you glorify God, one day God will glorify you. Remember how Moses reflected God's glory when he came down from God's mountain? The Bible says that one day the same thing will happen to every child of God. "When Christ, who is your life, appears, then you also will appear with him in glory" (Col. 3:4). You will receive what the Bible calls "an eternal weight of glory" (2 Cor. 4:17 KJV).

This is the doctrine of glorification. When you see Jesus in all his glory, you will be filled with as much glory as you can bear. Indeed, the Bible says that this is already starting to happen. "We, who with unveiled faces all reflect the Lord's glory, are being transformed into his likeness with ever-increasing glory, which comes from the Lord, who is the Spirit" (2 Cor. 3:18). The more you get into Christ, the more Christ gets into you, until eventually you are glorified all the way through. One day you will be totally glorious!

But God will not stop there. He has promised that he will not be satisfied until the whole earth is "filled with the knowledge of the glory of the LORD, as the waters cover the sea" (Hab. 2:14). God's ultimate purpose is to do everything for his own glory. When he discards this tired old world, he will fill the new heavens and the new earth with the full weight of his being. Then we will spend eternity praising him for all his glorious attributes. "For from him and through him and to him are all things. To him be the glory forever! Amen" (Rom. 11:36).

CHAPTER 2

GOD IS SPIRIT

The Story of the Messiah at the Well

⸻

God is spirit, and his worshipers must worship in spirit and in truth.

JOHN 4:24

The year was 1647. A hundred or more of Britain's most learned ministers and Bible scholars were meeting at Westminster Abbey in London to put the great doctrines of the Reformation down on paper. Their work proceeded steadily until they came to the divine attributes.

When it came to God, the Westminster divines hardly knew where to begin. For a while they tried—unsuccessfully—to write a suitable definition of deity. They became so discouraged that one of the members of the assembly finally suggested that they spend a season in prayer.

The young Scotsman George Gillespie (1613-1648) stood up and prayed, "O God, thou who art a spirit, infinite, eternal, and unchangeable in thy being, wisdom, power, holiness, justice, goodness, and truth—" At which point someone interrupted and said something like, "Wait a minute; someone ought to be writing this down!"[1]

There is some question as to whether or not that story is actually true. But there is little dispute about the quality of the Westminster Shorter Catechism's answer to the question, "What is God?" "God is a Spirit, infinite, eternal, and unchangeable in his being, wisdom, power, holiness, justice, goodness, and truth." It is a good answer to the most profound of all questions. James Benjamin Green once stated: "As a definition of indefinable Deity, the Shorter Catechism is unexcelled, unequaled [*sic*] by any other word of man."[2]

Although the fourth question in the catechism does not say everything that needs to be said about the attributes of God, it is an excellent place to begin. This question will provide the structure for the rest of this book. We will study, in turn, the spirituality, infinity, eternity, impassibility, aseity, omniscience, omnipotence, holiness, justice, goodness, and truth of God, as well as his love.

THE SPIRITUALITY OF GOD

God is a spirit. So begins the catechism. This is a direct quotation from holy Scripture: "God is spirit," or, as the King James Version has it, "God is *a* Spirit" (John 4:24). But what does it mean to say that God is spirit?

For one thing, it means that God does not have a body. In the previous study, we learned that the glory of God has something to do with how heavy he is. But God cannot be weighed on the scale at the doctor's office. He does not weigh anything in the literal, physical sense, because he does not have a body. He is not made out of matter at all.

"God is a Spirit," says the Catechism for Young Children, "and has not a body like men." His existence is spiritual. He has no visible shape or form. Thus, when the Bible speaks of God's "mighty arm and outstretched hand" (Deut. 7:19), or says, "your eyes saw my unformed body" (Ps. 139:16), it is using figures of speech. The essence of God is spiritual rather than physical.

Consider the alternative. If God did have a body, he would be limited by time and space. He could not be all-present or all-knowing. He would be tied down to one place at one time. He would be like a pagan idol chopped out of a block of wood (see Isa. 44), a created thing rather than the Creator. It is because he is spirit that God rules over and outside of time, space, and matter.

Many of the divine attributes depend on the fact that God is spirit. This is obviously true of his invisibility. If God had a physical existence, then he would be visible. It is true that he has sometimes revealed himself in a visible form, such as the glory-cloud Moses saw. Yet he himself is the King invisible (1 Tim. 1:17), "who lives in unapproachable light, whom no one has seen or can see" (1 Tim. 6:16). But only a spirit can be invisible.

Some people refuse to believe in God until they see him. Doubting Thomas was like that (John 20:25). So is the man at the nursing home where I sometimes preach. He is willing to come to our worship service, most of the time, but he always raises the same objection. With a big grin on his face, he says, "But I can't see God," as if that settles the argument.

I'm sad to say that the man's theology is limited by his eyeballs. Of course God cannot be seen! Invisibility is one of his essential attributes. We will never be able to look at God's goodness or figure out what color his justice is. But then I have never seen most of my wife's attributes either. I have never seen her love, for example, or gazed fondly at her kindness. Despite the fact that these qualities are invisible, they are nonetheless real.

The same is true of the attributes of God. The fact that he is invisible does not mean that he is nonexistent. The Catechism for Young Children has a nice way of putting it. "Can you see God?" "No, I cannot see God, but he always sees me." That answer is careful to assert the divine attribute of invisibility. But it is equally emphatic on the existence of God. Although God is unseen, he is not unseeing.

The fact that God is spirit shows how great he is. He does not have a body; therefore, he is not bound by time and space. He is invisible; therefore, he is not subject to our visual scrutiny.

Some aspects of his divine being remain forever beyond our reach, even beyond our comprehension.

The spirituality of God brings up an obvious question: What about Jesus Christ? God the Father may be a Spirit, and God the Holy Spirit obviously is, but doesn't God the Son have a body?

The answer is, yes, Jesus Christ does have a body. To deny his physical existence is an old and dangerous heresy. The Bible teaches that "the Word became flesh and made his dwelling among us" (John 1:14). Jesus had the kind of body that could eat and drink. He had the kind of body that could ride on a donkey or sail in a boat. Most important of all, Jesus had the kind of body that could suffer and die for sin.

Jesus Christ has two natures, however. Although he is one person, he has two natures—a divine nature and a human nature. His physical body is not part of his divine nature; his body belongs to his humanity. Therefore, his divine nature remains spiritual. Even God the Son is spirit. In the words of the apostle Paul, "the Lord . . . is the Spirit" (2 Cor. 3:18). Or again, "'The first man Adam became a living being'; the last Adam, a life-giving spirit" (1 Cor. 15:45).

THE WOMAN AT THE WELL

It is not easy to grasp the spirituality of God, but there is a story about it in the Bible that helps. The incident is sometimes called the story of the woman at the well, and it happened while Jesus was on his way from Judea to Galilee.

> So he came to a town in Samaria called Sychar, near the plot of ground Jacob had given to his son Joseph. Jacob's well was there, and Jesus, tired as he was from the journey, sat down by the well. It was about the sixth hour.
>
> When a Samaritan woman came to draw water, Jesus said to her, "Will you give me a drink?" (His disciples had gone into the town to buy food.) (John 4:5-8)

It is not surprising that Jesus was tired. It is a g
that he was a real human being with a real body
prising that the disciples had gone into town to buy ₁◡◡
fairly typical for them to be concerned about where their next
meal was coming from.

Otherwise, the whole encounter is full of surprises. For
starters, it was unusual for Jesus to meet alone like this with a
woman. When the disciples returned, they were "surprised to
find him talking with a woman" (v. 27a).

No doubt the woman's reputation added to their surprise. It
seems significant that she went to draw water alone (vv. 28-30).
The watering hole is always the center of village social life. Yet
this woman went there alone and in the heat of the day, rather
than in the cool of the evening. Very likely this was because of
her sexual sin. She went through husbands the way most people go through sandals (vv. 16-18). In all likelihood she was a
social outcast.

There they sat beside the well under the noonday sun—a
loose Samaritan woman and a sinless Jewish man. The
woman herself could hardly believe it. Jews were not in the
habit of sharing things like water buckets with Samaritans.
She said, "'You are a Jew and I am a Samaritan woman. How
can you ask me for a drink?' (For Jews do not associate with
Samaritans.)" (v. 9).

Actually, that was an understatement. The Jews hated the
Samaritans, a hatred the Samaritans returned with interest.
Their animosity toward one another was racially motivated. The
Samaritans were half-breeds, the product of intermarriage
between Jews and Gentiles (mainly Assyrians) after the fall of
Samaria in 722 B.C.

The Samaritans and the Jews had been enemies for centuries,
but the hostilities intensified in 128 B.C., when the Jewish king
John Hyrcanus attacked Samaria and destroyed their temple on
Mount Gerizim. The Samaritans responded with a vengeance,

attacking Jews on their way from Galilee to Jerusalem. They even piled human bones in the Jewish temple to defile it.[3]

The Jews despised the Samaritans for religious reasons as well as ethnic and political ones. Although they kept the Law of Moses, the Samaritans did not have the Psalms or the Prophets. By the time of Christ, some rabbis held that "to eat the bread of Samaritans was to eat pork, or to marry a Samaritan was to lie with a beast."[4] Whenever possible, devout Jews avoided Samaria entirely, crossing the Jordan River and going miles out of their way to get to Galilee.

There was nothing prejudiced about Jesus, however. He was not ashamed to go through Samaria or to associate with this woman. The way he treats her shows that "the people of God is to consist of all, whatever their race, their religious background or their moral standing may be, who acknowledge Jesus as the Saviour of the world, who have received from Him the life-giving Spirit, and who worship him in spirit and in truth."[5]

Jesus had come to die for the sins of Samaritans and to offer them the free gift of eternal life. Gesturing toward the well, he said, "'Everyone who drinks this water will be thirsty again, but whoever drinks the water I give him will never thirst. Indeed, the water I give him will become in him a spring of water welling up to eternal life'" (John 4:13-14).

Although Jesus was speaking spiritually, the woman was listening literally. Jesus was talking about the new life he came to give, but she thought he was talking about running water. Since she was more concerned with her physical needs than her spiritual needs, she wanted to know how she could tap into this water supply.

Speaking a little sarcastically, perhaps, "the woman said to him, 'Sir, give me this water so that I won't get thirsty and have to keep coming here to draw water'" (v. 15). After all, she wasted a great deal of time walking to the well, hauling up water buckets (Jacob's well was 100 feet deep), and then carrying her heavy water jar back to the village.

Jesus was happy to give the woman the water of life, but first she needed to confess her sins. "He told her, 'Go, call your husband and come back.' 'I have no husband,' she replied" (vv. 16-17a).

Technically, that was correct, but it was also misleading. "Jesus said to her, 'You are right when you say you have no husband. The fact is, you have had five husbands, and the man you now have is not your husband. What you have just said is quite true'" (vv. 17b-18).

THE MESSIAH AT THE WELL

It was time to change the subject, especially once Jesus mentioned her live-in boyfriend. "'Sir,' the woman said, 'I can see that you are a prophet. Our fathers worshiped on this mountain, but you Jews claim that the place where we must worship is in Jerusalem'" (vv. 19-20).

Somewhere along the way, the woman had learned that the best way to change the subject in the Middle East is to start talking about religion. Jerusalem or Gerizim?—that was *the* hot-button issue in those days. Today everyone knows where the temple belongs (Jerusalem); the only question is who has a right to worship on the mountain (Jews, Muslims, or Christians?). But back then, they were still arguing about which was the right mountain.

The Samaritans thought the only place to worship God was Mount Gerizim, which happened to be in (surprise, surprise) Samaria. This was based on their misreading of Scripture. Although thirteen different mountains are mentioned in the Pentateuch, the Samaritans thought these were simply thirteen different names for Gerizim. Noah's ark, Abraham's sacrifice, the Law of Moses—it all happened on Mount Gerizim.[6]

As you might imagine, the Samaritans were rather proud of their mountain. One ancient text tells how

> Rabbi Ishmael ben Jose was going up to Jerusalem to pray. He was walking past a plane tree [by Gerizim] where a Samaritan found him. He said to him, "Where are you going?" He answered, "I am going up to Jerusalem to pray." The former said, "Would it not be better for you to pray in this blessed mountain rather than in that dunghill?"[7]

Although she was a little more polite about it, the woman at the well was asking Jesus the same question.

In his answer Jesus mentions three kinds of worship.[8] The first is *ignorant* worship, which is what the Samaritans offered to God. "'You Samaritans worship what you do not know'" (John 4:22a).

When it came to worship, the Samaritans did not know what they were doing. They were sincere. They were trying to worship God as well as they knew how. But they were ignorant. The only Scripture they had was the Law of Moses, and they were misinterpreting that. Therefore, their worship was regulated by the traditions of men rather than by the Word of God. They worshiped God in the wrong way and at the wrong place.

The second kind of worship is *intelligent* worship. It has become popular to think that it does not matter how you worship, as long as you are sincere. Jesus, however, did not hesitate to draw a clear line between acceptable and unacceptable worship. Here he came down squarely on the side of the Jews (which is not surprising, since Jesus was a Jew). "'We worship what we do know,'" Jesus said, "'for salvation is from the Jews'" (v. 22b).

When it came to worship, the Jews knew what they were doing. They were not caught up in superstitions like worshiping on Mount Gerizim. They had the Prophets as well as the Law.

Thus they worshiped God the only proper way, offering sacrifices to him at the temple in Jerusalem.

Then Jesus mentions a third kind of worship, which might be called *innovative* worship. It was something totally new, as far as worship was concerned. What this new worship emphasized was the spirituality of God. "Jesus declared, 'Believe me, woman, a time is coming when you will worship the Father neither on this mountain nor in Jerusalem. . . . Yet a time is coming and has now come when the true worshipers will worship the Father in spirit and truth, for they are the kind of worshipers the Father seeks'" (vv. 21, 23).

Jesus was about to end the argument between the Jews and the Samaritans once and for all. As the Samaritans shortly were to discover, the Messiah would be the Savior of the world (v. 42). With his coming, God's people would worship neither on Gerizim nor in Jerusalem. After all, God is spirit. Therefore, his people would worship him everywhere in spirit and in truth.

That time was coming. In fact, the punch line of the story is that it had practically arrived already. "The woman said, 'I know that Messiah' (called Christ) 'is coming. When he comes, he will explain everything to us'" (v. 25). She was trying to procrastinate, but the Christ had already come! "Then Jesus declared, 'I who speak to you am he'" (v. 26). It turns out that this is not the story of the woman at the well after all. It is the story of the Messiah at the well.

Jesus is the Savior God promised to send. Literally, what he says is, "I am, the one speaking to you." In other words, Jesus is one and the same as the great "I AM," the Lord God of Israel who spoke to Moses from the burning bush (Ex. 3:14). Now that he has come to take away the sins of the world, God is to be worshiped—not in Jerusalem or on Mount Gerizim—but everywhere in spirit and in truth.

WORSHIP IN SPIRIT

What does it mean to worship God in spirit? Because we live in a material world, it is hard for us to understand the spirituality of God. Yet the truth that God is spirit has several practical implications for Christian worship.

It means, first of all, that God may be worshiped in any and every place (just as the Old Testament promised; Mal. 1:11). In the past, God located his presence at the temple in Jerusalem. He could be worshiped elsewhere, of course. There were synagogues in Nazareth, Capernaum, and all over Israel. But there was something special about God's holy presence at the temple, where atonement was offered for sin.

Now Jesus has made the temple obsolete. He has offered atonement for sin once and for all by dying on the cross. Furthermore, he has sent his Spirit to live in the heart of everyone who believes in him. Because God's Spirit lives in us, we have immediate access to God. Through the indwelling presence of the Holy Spirit, *Jesus* is our place of worship.

That is why Christians need not be very fussy about where they worship. In the words of the poet William Cowper (1731-1800):

> *Jesus, where e'er your people meet,*
> *there they behold your mercy seat;*
> *Where e'er they seek you, you are found,*
> *and ev'ry place is hallowed ground.*

Christians worship everywhere. They meet in little chapels and great cathedrals, in storefronts and warehouses. Alone and in groups, they praise God in the valleys as well as on the mountaintops. They gather for worship in the city, the country, the woods, and the desert. Through the Holy Spirit, Christians worship God anywhere and everywhere. What makes this possible, of course, is the spirituality of God.

In order for anyone to worship God in spirit, a spiritual

change must take place. This is the second part of what it means to worship God in spirit. Worship is a spiritual matter. It takes a spiritual person to worship a spiritual God. Until God's Spirit changes your life, you cannot worship God properly at all.

Has a spiritual change taken place in your life?

Although the details are different for every person, it generally happens like this. God sends his Spirit into your heart. The Holy Spirit convinces you that you are a sinner in need of God's forgiveness. This is called "repentance." Next God's Spirit helps you believe that Jesus died for your sins. This is called "faith," and it leads to eternal life. When you repent for your sins and put your faith in Jesus Christ, you become a whole new person spiritually.

Every autumn the Bible school superintendent holds a dinner for the Sunday school teachers at Tenth Presbyterian Church in Philadelphia. One year the superintendent asked each teacher to give a short testimony of coming to faith in Jesus Christ.

The testimonies were moving. Many of the teachers had prayed to receive Christ with their parents when they were children. Some were converted through Christian radio. One man was led to Christ by a neighbor after his parents had separated. One woman sat up in the balcony of a church, listening to a sermon and saying, "This is what I have been waiting to hear all my life." Still another woman became a Christian when she overheard someone telling her roommate about Jesus Christ.

Every testimony was different, a unique history of the power and grace of God in the salvation of a sinner. But every testimony was also the same. The same spiritual change had taken place in every heart. Each one had confessed his or her sins, believed in Jesus Christ, and become a new spiritual person. From that time on, each one was enabled to worship God in spirit and in truth.

Finally, to worship God in spirit is to worship him in a spiritual way. God is not concerned about the "where" of worship, but he is concerned about the "who" and the "how." You must be a spiritual person, and you must worship in a spiritual way.

The reason God must be worshiped in a spiritual way is because he is spirit. God can only be worshiped as he is. Because he is spirit, there is no other way to worship him except in spirit. This is the third great "must" in the Gospel of John.[9] "'You must be born again'" (3:7). "'The Son of Man must be lifted up'" (v. 14). "'God is spirit, and his worshipers must worship in spirit and in truth'" (John 4:24). There is no other way to worship God except in spirit. It is as necessary as the new birth or the cross of Christ. Worship is spiritual because God is spirit.

When Jesus told the woman at the well that she must worship in spirit, he was not speaking about the Holy Spirit as much as he was speaking about her spirit, the inward life of her soul. The two are closely related, of course, since it is God's Spirit who enables our spirits to worship. But what Jesus wanted to emphasize is that we must worship God inwardly as well as outwardly.

It is easy to get caught up in the outward acts of worship, the routines of standing up and sitting down to sing and to pray. However, just because your body occupies space in a church pew one hour a week does not mean that you worship God. It is also easy to become distracted from worship, especially when one is spending time alone with God. But real worship is the engagement of the entire soul in the adoration of God. The mind, the heart, and the will are all directed toward his glory.

It is not easy to worship a spiritual God. In order to do it at all, we need spiritual help. A favorite prayer of the great German Reformer Philipp Melanchthon (1497-1560) went like this: "Lord, inflame my soul with thy Holy Spirit."[10] That is an excellent prayer for every Christian to offer when entering a house of worship or sitting down to read and pray in private devotion. For only when our spirits are inflamed with God's Spirit are we able to worship God—who is spirit—in a spiritual way.

CHAPTER 3

GOD IS EVERYWHERE

The Story of Jonah and the Great Escape

———✦———

Where can I go from your Spirit?
Where can I flee from your presence? If I go up to the heavens,
you are there; if I make my bed in the depths, you are there.

PSALM 139:7-8

There is a children's book about the presence of God called *God Is with Me*. It is delightful to hold a very small person on your lap and read from it these words:

> *My God always sees me.*
> *He sees me when I sit down and when I stand up.*
> *He sees me when I go outside.*
> *And God sees me when I go to bed.*
> *God is too wonderful for me to see Him now . . .*
>   *but He sees me!*
> *My God is always with me.*
> *If I go UP, He is with me.*
> *If I go DOWN, He is with me!*
> *If I wake up quietly, before everyone else . . .*
>   *even then my God is with me!*
> *If I swim to the bottom of the sea . . . God is with me!*
> *When it is so dark that I cannot see, God can see*
>   *and He is with me.*
> *God made me wonderfully, and He loves me.*
> *Tomorrow, when I wake up, God will still be with me!*[1]

Those words are a paraphrase of Psalm 139, a psalm David wrote about the infinite knowledge and presence of God. "'Where can I go from your Spirit?'" David asks. "'Where can I flee from your presence?'" (Ps. 139:7). These are questions we began to answer in the previous chapter. God is worshiped in every place because he is spirit.

GOD'S INFINITE PRESENCE

In this chapter we are trying to understand what it means that God is an *infinite* spirit. He is infinite in every respect, of course. He is infinite in wisdom, power, goodness, and so forth. But God is also infinite in his presence. He is not confined or limited to any one place. His essence is included in no physical place. At the same time, there is no place from which his essence is excluded. God is present in all places at once.

Theologians use several words to describe God's infinite presence. Sometimes they say he is "omnipresent," meaning that he is all-present. Sometimes they speak of God's "ubiquity," which is a fancy of saying that God is everywhere.

Another term often used to describe God is "immensity." The immensity of God does not mean that he is big, or even extra, extra large. He does not have a size at all. The Puritan Thomas Watson stated that trying to measure God's presence is like asking a mathematician to span the globe with a geometric compass.[2] How can you measure an infinite spirit?

It is impossible for us to wrap our finite minds around God's infinite presence. We are finite beings bound by time and space. We exist in one and only one place at one time. "Well, I can't be two places at once, can I?" we say. But God does not have that limitation. The medieval theologians thus compared him to a circle whose center is everywhere and whose circumference is nowhere. In other words, God does not have any boundaries.

Because God is an infinite spirit, he is everywhere. And he is always close at hand. "He is not far from each one of us. 'For in him we live and move and have our being'" (Acts 17:27-28). God's close presence is not simply or even primarily spatial; rather, it is personal and relational. The whole of life is lived within the atmosphere of the God "who fills everything in every way" (Eph. 1:23).

To help understand the fullness of God's presence, consider this illustration from A. W. Tozer:

> God fills heaven and earth just as the ocean fills a bucket which has been submerged in it a mile down. The bucket is full of the ocean, but the ocean surrounds the bucket in all directions. So when God says He fills heaven and earth, He does. But heaven and earth are submerged in God, and all space is too.[3]

God "fills everything in every way" (Eph. 1:23). He is all, and in all, and all is in him.

We have already mentioned that all the divine attributes are expressed in Jesus Christ. But what about God's infinite presence? How can the incarnate Son of God be omnipresent?

The Bible clearly teaches that Jesus Christ is now in heaven. "After he had provided purification for sins, he sat down at the right hand of the Majesty in heaven" (Heb. 1:3). To this very day "Christ is seated at the right hand of God" (Col. 3:1). His resurrection body is located in heaven. It is a glorified body (1 Peter 1:21), and a spiritual body (1 Cor. 15:44-45), but it is still a body. It will remain a body for all eternity because Jesus Christ will never discard his human nature.

Nevertheless, there is a sense in which Jesus is infinitely present in the world—in his divine nature. He is called "Immanuel—which means 'God with us'" (Matt. 1:23). He is with us when we meet as the church, for he told his disciples, "'Where two or three come together in my name, there am I with them'" (Matt.

18:20). The omnipresence of Christ enabled Paul to give a charge to Timothy, not only in "the presence of God," but also "of Christ Jesus" (2 Tim. 4:1). Christ is with us. Indeed, he has promised to be with us "always, to the very end of the age" (Matt. 28:20b).

Christ is also in us. The New Testament often teaches that every Christian is in Christ (e.g., Rom. 8:1; 2 Cor. 5:17). But it also teaches that Christ is in every Christian. He dwells "in your hearts through faith" (Eph. 3:17). "Christ in you [is] the hope of glory" (Col. 1:27).

How can Christ be in heaven and in us at the same time? In his divine nature, the Son always has been, is now, and always will be all-present. But what about his human nature?

The mysterious presence of Christ's human nature has to do with the work of the Holy Spirit. After Christ ascended to heaven, he sent his Spirit into the world. Now the Holy Spirit is the one who brings Christ to us. Although the Son is absent from us in body, he is present with us in the Spirit. Thus the presence of Christ in the Christian, in worship, and in the sacrament of the Lord's Supper is a spiritual presence.

These are high mysteries. In the end all explanations and analogies fail. The attribute of omnipresence is unique. Because it belongs to God alone, it is beyond our comprehension.

When the famous evangelical preacher John Wesley (1703-1791) tried to explain God's presence, he had to admit that "this subject is far too vast to be comprehended by the narrow limits of human understanding. We can only say, the great God, the eternal, the almighty Spirit, is as unbounded in His presence, as in His duration and power."[4]

THE GREAT ESCAPE

There is a story about God's infinite presence in the Bible. It is the story of Jonah and the great escape.

God had noticed that the city of Nineveh was in a bad way. Nineveh—the capital of Assyria, the greatest superpower in the world—had become an immoral and degenerate city. God had the right to dispose of it as he pleased. But God had a heart for the city, and in his grace he decided to save Nineveh.

God's plan for saving the city began with recruiting Jonah to go on a short-term missions trip. "The word of the LORD came to Jonah son of Amittai: 'Go to the great city of Nineveh and preach against it, because its wickedness has come up before me'" (Jonah 1:1-2). Literally, the sins of Nineveh were in God's "presence" (remember, he is all-present).

Just about the last thing Jonah wanted to do was go and hold a Bible conference in Nineveh, the place the prophet Nahum called "the city of blood" (Nah. 3:1). Jonah's reluctance may have had something to do with the fact that it was so far away or that he did not want to go to the inner city. It almost certainly had to do with his ethnic prejudice.

The Assyrians were the sworn enemies of the Jews, not to mention practically everyone else in the world. Jonah wanted nothing to do with evangelizing his enemies. Preacher and author Ray Bakke says he was "wrapping the gospel in his flag."[5] By the end of Jonah's book, it becomes clear that he simply did not want God to save those foreigners (Jonah 4:1-2).

For this reason, when God said, "Go!" Jonah said, "No!" "But Jonah ran away from the LORD and headed for Tarshish. He went down to Joppa, where he found a ship bound for that port. After paying the fare, he went aboard and sailed for Tarshish to flee from the LORD" (Jonah 1:3).

Tarshish, as it happens, is in the opposite direction from Nineveh. Way in the opposite direction. Today it would be like going to Oahu instead of Manhattan. God told Jonah to head east, but the young man decided to go west, through the straits of Gibraltar, to the distant coast of Spain. With any luck, by the time the ship visited all its ports of call, his cruise would last as long as a year.

Jonah was embarking on a long disobedience in the wrong direction. It was going to be an expensive sabbatical. Ships bound for Tarshish were the ocean liners of biblical times. At the very least, Jonah went down to the harbor and bought a one-way ticket to the farthest possible destination. The renowned pastor Donald Grey Barnhouse noticed the humor in this: "When you run away from the Lord, you never get to where you are going, and you always pay your own fare. On the other hand, when you go the Lord's way, you always get to where you are going, and he pays the fare."[6]

There is a possibility, however, that Jonah did more than pay his fare. He seems to have bought the whole boat. The Hebrew text does not say that Jonah "paid his fare." It actually says that he "paid her price," which may mean the price of the whole ship.[7]

Jewish commentators have always taught that Jonah spent a fortune on his great escape. These days most missionaries spend a lot of time raising their support, but before you could say "Nineveh Inland Mission," Jonah had squandered everything he had. By the time he bought his boat, he probably did not have enough money to get to Nineveh, even if he wanted to, which he most emphatically did not.

By going his own way, Jonah put God to the test. He tested not only God's patience, but also his presence. Here the biblical language is very explicit. The *New Revised Standard Version* brings it out twice in verse 3 and again in verse 10: "Jonah ran away from the *presence* of the LORD." Jonah's example shows in the clearest way that sin means separation from God.

Jonah was conducting an experiment. He was doing lab work in practical theology. In Psalm 139 David asked where he could go from God's Spirit, how he could flee from God's presence. Jonah had heard David's answers, in all likelihood, but he wanted to carry out his own independent research. He told any-one who cared to ask that he was "running away from the pres-ence of the LORD" (Jonah 1:10 NRSV).

The results of Jonah's experiment were rather unexpected. "Then the LORD sent a great wind on the sea, and such a vio-lent storm arose that the ship threatened to break up. All the sailors were afraid and each cried out to his own god. And they threw the cargo into the sea to lighten the ship" (Jonah 1:4-5a). God was present all right, present in the storm with power and might. Literally, he "hurled" the storm at Jonah.

It must have been some storm. The Hebrew word used here for "sailor" is not the word for men who are still trying to find their "sea legs." They were grizzled veterans of wind and wave. In English we would say they were "old salts." But even these old men of the sea were terrified. Desperately, they cried out to their gods and threw their precious cargo into the stormy deeps.

These sailors did not know the living God, but at least they had the sense to pray when they got into trouble. They prayed first, before they started to jettison their cargo. They prayed even though they did not know whether or not their prayers would be answered.

Meanwhile, where was old Jonah? "Jonah had gone below deck, where he lay down and fell into a deep sleep" (v. 5b). He was sleeping through the storm, oblivious to the danger he was in, both nautically and spiritually. "The captain went to him and said, 'How can you sleep? Get up and call on your god! Maybe he will take notice of us, and we will not perish'" (v. 6). Since the captain had ordered all hands on deck, he was amazed to catch Jonah napping.

The captain obviously had his doubts about the usefulness of prayer. The only gods he knew were the gods of the pagans, and they were extremely unreliable. In his experience gods might or might not pay attention to your prayers. They might be busy somewhere else. You could never be sure because they were not all-present. The irony is that it took such a pagan to teach Jonah to pray.

When the pagan gods failed to answer, the sailors cast lots to figure out who was responsible for the storm (Jonah 1:7). The lot fell on Jonah, of course, at which point the sailors wanted to know who he was, what he was doing, and especially what God he served. His answer terrified them. "He answered, 'I am a Hebrew and I worship the LORD, the God of heaven, who made the sea and the land'" (v. 9).

It was obvious that Jonah's God was no local deity. He was the Supreme God who rules the heavens, the sea, and the dry land. In other words, he rules everything and is present everywhere, even on board a little ship bound for Tarshish.

The sea was getting so rough that the sailors knew something had to be done. The last thing they wanted to do was make Jonah's God any angrier than he already was, so they did their best to row Jonah back to land. Finally, the sea grew so wild that nothing else could be done. "They took Jonah and threw him overboard, and the raging sea grew calm" (v. 15).

PRESENT IN JUDGMENT

This story is full of practical lessons about God's infinite presence. The first lesson is that it is impossible to run away from God's judgment. There is not one single place in the whole universe for a sinner to escape from the wrath of God.

Jonah tried to run, but he could not hide from God's presence. God saw Jonah's sin. He watched him go down to the harbor in Joppa, book his passage, and set sail for the western islands. God was present when the storm began to rise on the surface of the sea. He was present, too, when Jonah was tossed over the side of the ship. The storm continued right up until the moment Jonah splashed into the sea. God was present in judgment.

Since the first sin of Adam, human beings have been trying

(and failing) to cover up their sin. "'Can anyone hide in secret places so that I cannot see him?' declares the LORD. 'Do not I fill heaven and earth?' declares the LORD" (Jer. 23:24). In the words of the Haitian liberator Toussaint-L'Ouverture (1743-1803), "I cannot see everything, but nothing escapes God."

There is no such thing as a secret sin. Every sin comes under the direct scrutiny of the omnipresent God. Not even the privacy of your own mind is private. The Bible says that on the day of judgment "God will judge men's secrets through Jesus Christ" (Rom. 2:16). It is a fearful thought, yet true. All our attempts to cover up our sin will ultimately fail. Sin cannot escape God's notice.

There is a sense in which every sin is really a denial of the presence of God. As you reflect on your conduct, at least one or two sins must come to mind that you wish before God you had never committed. Probably you never would have committed them if Jesus Christ had been standing right next to you. But Christ *was* with you when you committed those sins. He was present there as he is everywhere else. By sinning, however, you were doing your best to deny the reality of his presence.

It follows that few things are more helpful in restraining sin than a keen awareness of God's constant presence. There are many sins we commit in private that we would never dream of committing if others were present. President William Jefferson Clinton gave an insight into the nature of sin when he was caught in adultery. "I did what people do when they do the wrong thing," he said. "I tried to do it where nobody else was looking at it."[8]

If you want to keep away from sin, remember how impossible it is to escape God's notice. Never live as though God does not exist. Practice "the presence of God," as Brother Lawrence termed it.[9] Speak to the Lord frequently throughout the day. Remember that everything you say, do, or even think is said, done, and thought in the infinite presence of a holy God.

PRESENT IN GRACE

However, the omnipresence of God does not simply provoke fear; it also offers comfort. A second lesson to be learned from Jonah is that you cannot run away from God's grace, any more than you can run away from his judgment.

God was present in grace for the sailors in Jonah's boat. God heard their prayer for forgiveness (Jonah 1:14), for he "is near to all who call on him. . . . he hears their cry and saves them" (Ps. 145:18-19).

The last thing the Bible says about those old sailors is that they came to worship God in the biblical way. As the sea grew calm, they had a powerful sense of his presence. As the sky cleared and the waves lapped gently against the boat, "the men greatly feared the LORD, and they offered a sacrifice to the LORD and made vows to him" (Jonah 1:16).

Like the sailors, Jonah received God's ever-present grace. Indeed, he could not escape it.

The prophet used poetry to describe his experience. At first he felt as if he were drowning:

> *"You hurled me into the deep,*
>   *into the very heart of the seas,*
>   *and the currents swirled about me;*
> *all your waves and breakers*
>   *swept over me. . . ."* (2:3)

Jonah fought to keep his head above water, but then he got tangled in seaweed and started to go under.

> *"The engulfing waters threatened me,*
>   *the deep surrounded me;*
>   *seaweed was wrapped around my head.*
> *To the roots of the mountains I sank down;*
>   *the earth beneath barred me in forever."* (2:5-6a)

By the time Jonah finally asked for God's mercy, he thought he was a dead man. His life was "ebbing away" (v. 7), and he was about to become forever entombed in the deep.

> *"In my distress I called to the LORD,*
> *and he answered me.*
> *From the depths of the grave I called for help,*
> *and you listened to my cry." (2:2)*

Jonah prayed from the entrails of death.

As he floated down, down to the bottom of the sea, he had a terrifying thought: His experiment had succeeded; he had actually managed to escape from God's presence. He said, "'I have been banished from your sight'" (2:4).

But Jonah could not escape God's ever-present grace. God was there when he was thrown off the deck of the ship. He was there to provide a great fish (possibly a whale) to swallow Jonah (1:17). Even in the belly of a whale at the bottom of the sea, God was there to hear Jonah's prayer.

> *"But you brought my life up from the pit,*
> *O LORD my God.*
> *When my life was ebbing away,*
> *I remembered you, LORD,*
> *and my prayer rose to you,*
> *to your holy temple." (2:6b-7)*

God heard Jonah from his heavenly throne because the Lord was right there in the depths of the sea. And God gave Jonah his grace, or "lovingkindness," as it is called (v. 8 KJV). Jonah could not run away from God's grace. By that irresistible grace he was saved from death.

When people hear the story of Jonah, they are usually interested in what was happening in the whale. But the real miracle was what was happening in Jonah![10] He was learning to trust in the omnipresent God.

Once he had been saved by grace, Jonah was able to speak the words of David's psalm from his own experience:

> *Where can I go from your Spirit?*
> *Where can I flee from your presence?*
> *If I go up to the heavens, you are there;*
> *if I make my bed in the depths, you are there.*
> *If I rise on the wings of the dawn,*
> *if I settle on the far side of the sea,*
> *even there your hand will guide me,*
> *your right hand will hold me fast.* (Ps. 139:7-10)

It is significant that the Hebrew word *Sheol* is used by both David ("the depths," Ps. 139:8) and Jonah ("the grave," Jonah 2:2). For the Hebrews, Sheol was the place of death. The fact that Jonah was in a kind of Sheol for three days and three nights is symbolic of the mercy God has shown to sinners through the resurrection of Jesus Christ. Jesus told the Pharisees they would be given this sign: "'For as Jonah was three days and three nights in the belly of a huge fish, so the Son of Man will be three days and three nights in the heart of the earth'" (Matt. 12:40).

Jonah was the illustration; Jesus is the resurrected reality. After he was crucified, Jesus remained in the heart of the earth for three days and three nights. But God is everywhere, even in the grave itself, and by his Spirit he raised Jesus from the dead. Now the same power by which God raised Jesus from the dead—the power of his ever-present grace—is available to everyone who trusts in him for salvation from sin and death.

Have you received this grace? Perhaps you keep high moral standards, like the sailors on Jonah's ship, yet you have not given your heart to God. Or perhaps you are more like Jonah, a believer going your own rebellious way. Whoever you are, God's grace is near to you, even nearer than you think.

Francis Thompson wrote a poem called "The Hound of Heaven" about being pursued by God's grace. The poem begins with the poet trying to escape from a stranger in hot pursuit:

> *I fled Him, down the nights and down the days;*
> *I fled Him, down the arches of the years;*
> *I fled Him, down the labyrinthine ways*
> *Of my own mind; and in the midst of tears*
> *I hid from Him, and under running laughter.*

The poet runs and runs until he finally tires of the chase and stops. There, beside him in the darkness, is a presence. He discovers that the stranger he has been running from all this time is God himself, "The Hound of Heaven," who says, "Ah, fondest, blindest, weakest, I am He Whom thou seekest!"[11]

Has God's grace tracked you down yet? Perhaps you have been running around looking for meaning and joy in life. But is it possible that the whole time you have been running away from God? If only you would stop for a moment and listen, you would find that he is right next to you, waiting for you to invite him into your life. Do not run away from God; run toward him.

PRESENT IN THE CALL

The final lesson to be learned from Jonah and his great escape attempt is that once you have received God's grace, you cannot run away from God's call.

It would have been much better for Jonah to obey God in the first place. God called him to go to Nineveh, and one way or another, God was going to make sure he got there. Ray Bakke likes to say that "Jonah bought the one-way ticket, but God gave him the round trip."[12]

Unfortunately for Jonah, when he was finally ready to obey God's calling for his life, he found himself lying in a pool of vomit on the beach (Jonah 2:10). In the providence of God, that is what he needed to experience before he could be fruitful in ministry.

If you belong to God by the grace of Jesus Christ, you cannot run away from God's calling. You may not want that calling. You may try to delay that calling. You may even try to reject that calling. But eventually God will have his way with you. There is no way to escape it. God will not let you go.

When you answer God's call, you will discover that the same God who is all-present in judgment and all-present in grace will be all-present to help you. If you go where God wants you to go, he will go with you in all the comfort and help of his loving presence. This is his unbreakable promise: "'Never will I leave you; never will I forsake you'" (Heb. 13:5).

The promise of God's presence means that God is with you for all of life's emergencies. He is "an ever-present help in trouble" (Ps. 46:1). Furthermore, wherever God is present, he is present in all the fullness of his divine attributes. As the Puritan Stephen Charnock (1628-1680) explained:

> This presence is not without the special presence of all his attributes. . . . It is not a piece of God is here, and another parcel there, but God in his whole essence and perfections; in his wisdom to guide us, his power to protect and support us, his mercy to pity us, his fullness to refresh us, and his goodness to relieve us.[13]

One might say that wherever God is, he is "all there."

Best of all, the presence of God will remain with you after all your troubles are over. This is the glorious promise from the end of the Bible: "'Now the dwelling of God is with men, and he will live with them. They will be his people, and God himself will be with them and be their God'" (Rev. 21:3). To be in heaven is to be with God, and to be with God is to be in heaven, for in his presence there is fullness of joy (Ps. 16:11).

One man who trusted the promise of God's constant presence was Patrick (c. 390–c. 461), the first Christian missionary to Ireland. Patrick faced many dangers during his lifetime, some of them at sea. As a teenager he was kidnapped by pirates and forced into slavery. Once he became a missionary, he was opposed by pagans, witches, and barbarians.

In spite of all these dangers, Patrick took courage from God's infinite presence. Every day he offered the prayer that came to be known as "St. Patrick's Breastplate."

> *Christ with me, Christ before me, Christ behind me,*
> *Christ in me, Christ beneath me, Christ above me,*
> *Christ on my right, Christ on my left,*
> *Christ when I lie down, Christ when I sit down,*
>   *Christ when I arise.*

Wherever we go, God will go with us, for he is everywhere.

CHAPTER 4

NOW TO THE KING ETERNAL

The Story of the Boastful King of Babylon

—❧—

Now to the King eternal, immortal, invisible, the only God,
be honor and glory for ever and ever. Amen.

1 TIMOTHY 1:17

Nothing lasts forever. This is the undeniable lesson of history. All the great civilizations of the past have tumbled to the ground. Egypt fell to Assyria. The Assyrians were overrun by the Babylonians. The wisdom of Athens was followed by the might of Rome, which in turn was sacked by the barbarians. The Holy Roman Empire was fragmented into the nations of Europe, which grew in strength until they conquered the kingdoms of the Americas.

All that is left of those ancient kingdoms is the ruins. The glories of Egypt are covered with sand. Nearly all that remains of Assyria is a pair of enormous winged gates in the British Museum. Old Rome has been reduced to a collection of old coins, broken statues, and fallen buildings. The remains of the Aztecs, the Incas, and the Mayas are being analyzed by archaeologists.

The same fate awaits the United States of America, the greatest superpower the world has ever known. This empire, too, will disappear, at least at the return of Christ, if not sooner. And it may be sooner. The day may come when American currency is a relic in a museum and when tourists pick their way through the ruins of the capital, trying to imagine what the Washington Monument looked like when it was still standing.

Nothing lasts forever.

THE EVERLASTING FATHER

Except God. God will last forever because he is not a thing. He is not made of matter at all. He is an infinite spirit, infinite in time as well as space. He is the one Abraham knew as "the Eternal God" (Gen. 21:33), whom Isaiah called "the everlasting God" (Isa. 40:28) and Jeremiah worshiped as "the eternal King" (Jer. 10:10).

Some things have both a beginning and an end. The life span of a fruit fly, for example. A concert. The baseball season. A lunch break. Each of these events begins at a specific moment in time, continues, and then comes to an end. Whether the end is marked by death, an encore, an out, or a bell, the event does not continue indefinitely.

Other things have a beginning but no end. The angels are like that. They are created beings, and to be created is to be created in time. But the angels will never run out of time because they were created to be immortal. The same can be said about the souls of human beings. Every soul comes into being at conception, the moment human life begins. But God has given us souls that can never die. We have a beginning without an end.

God alone has neither a beginning nor an end. He is not in time at all. He cannot be timed. He is never early or late. He never clocks in, and he never clocks out. He is outside of time altogether. He is eternal by his very nature.

Time began only when God created the world. But even before creation, there was already God. The first words of the Bible confront us with God's awesome eternity. "In the beginning God" (Gen. 1:1). Here is what A. W. Pink said about these words:

There was time, if "time" it could be called, when God, in the unity of His nature, dwelt all alone. "In the beginning, God." There was no heaven, where His glory is now particularly manifested. There was no earth to engage His attention. There were no angels to hymn His praises; no universe to be upheld by the word of His power. There was nothing, no one, but God; and that, not for a day, a year, or an age, but "from everlasting."[1]

God exists from eternity past. His existence also extends into the future. God is, he was, and he is to come (Rev. 1:8). He "lives for ever and ever" (Rev. 10:6). "Your years will never end," writes the psalmist (Ps. 102:27b). "From everlasting to everlasting you are God" (Ps. 90:2). As the great Scottish preacher Thomas Boston (1676-1732) put it, "He was from everlasting before time, and will remain unto everlasting when time shall be no more; without beginning of life or end of days."[2]

Not only is God eternal, but everything associated with him is eternal. His name will be great forever (1 Chron. 17:24). His throne is an eternal throne (Ps. 93:2). His covenant is an everlasting covenant (Gen. 17:7). His words will never pass away (Matt. 24:35). Best of all, his love endures forever (1 Chron. 16:34).

It is hard enough for us to understand time, let alone eternity. Augustine (354-430) said, "If no man will ask me the question what time is, I know well enough what it is; but if any ask me what it is, I know not how to explain it."[3] When it comes to eternity, we do not know what it is even when we are *not* being asked to explain it.

We spend all of our time in time. We always want to know what time it is. We are ever conscious of the fact that time is slipping away. We spend our whole existence living from moment to moment.

But God is not like that. He does not have a succession of moments. The fact that God is eternal means that he transcends time. It is not as if God's existence is like our existence, only longer; rather, God lives beyond time. That is why his perspective on time is so different from ours. "With the Lord a day is like a thousand years, and a thousand years are like a day" (2 Peter 3:8).

To what can we compare the eternity of God? The medieval theologians—Boethius (c. 480-524), among others—said that human history is like a journey around the base of a mountain. God sits on top of the mountain and sees all of history happen all at once. It is not past or future to him, only present. God does not have a past or a future—only an eternal present.

The fact that God is eternal does not mean that he is immobile. To say that he lives in the eternal present makes it sound as if he is almost paralyzed. But God is not static. He is the living God, full of energy and force. The Dutch theologian Herman Bavinck (1854-1921) says, "we have an analogy of God's eternity in the abundant and exuberant life of the cheerful laborer, who never even considers time, and whose days and hours speed by."[4]

Occasionally, human beings lose track of time. We become so absorbed in our work or play that we stop watching the clock altogether. Experts on human performance call this "flow."[5] It is when we are in flow that we are most productive. But God is in flow all the time, thoroughly and timelessly engaged with his creation.

The British author C. S. Lewis (1898-1963) once tried to explain the eternity of God like this: Imagine an infinite sheet of paper stretching endlessly in every direction. Then imagine taking a pencil and drawing a line only one inch long. That line represents the entire history of the universe. The moment the pencil touched the paper was the beginning of time, and the moment it was lifted off was the end of time. That little line is surrounded in every direction by the vast and infinite eternity of God.[6]

God's eternity is more than we can understand. What we can understand is that eternity is of the very essence of God. It is essential to all his other attributes.

Imagine, for a moment, a god who possessed all the other divine attributes except eternity. He would be good, but not for all time. He would have power, but eventually he would have a power outage. Worst of all, his love would not endure forever. Such a temporary god would be no god at all.

This shows how all the attributes of God hang together. They are not abstract principles that can be isolated from one another. They are essential characteristics integrated into the personality of the triune God. Eternity is of the very "Godness" of God. It is what makes all his other divine attributes infinite.

A LIMITED MONARCHY

There are not many stories about the eternity of God in the Bible. How could there be? Stories take place in time. They always have a beginning, a middle, and an end. But the divine attribute of eternity means that God does not have a beginning, a middle, or an end.

There is one story, however, that teaches something about the eternity of God. It is the story of the boastful king of Babylon.

Babylon was the greatest city in the world, renowned for its wealth and learning, situated on the mighty Euphrates River. Its walls were 300 feet high, 75 feet wide, and 60 miles in circumference.[7] On each side of the city were twenty-five bronze gates. At the center of it all was the park where the king lived, six miles around.

The king's name was Nebuchadnezzar. One day he went for a stroll on the roof of his royal palace. From that vantage point he could see the Hanging Gardens, one of the Seven Wonders of the Ancient World. As he gazed out over the city, he realized that he was lord of all that he surveyed. "He said, 'Is not this the great Babylon I have built as the royal residence, by my mighty power and for the glory of my majesty?'" (Dan. 4:30).

What Nebuchadnezzar said was largely true. Babylon was a

great city, it was his royal residence, and it had been built by his power and glory. In some measure, he himself possessed the royal attributes of power, glory, and majesty.

Nebuchadnezzar was not sovereign, however, and his kingship was not eternal. No sooner had the braggy king of Babylon boasted of his might than his kingdom was taken away. The words were still on his lips when a voice came from heaven, "'This is what is decreed for you, King Nebuchadnezzar: Your royal authority has been taken from you. You will be driven away from people and will live with the wild animals; you will eat grass like cattle. Seven times will pass by for you until you acknowledge that the Most High is sovereign over the kingdoms of men and gives them to anyone he wishes.'"

Immediately what had been said about Nebuchadnezzar was fulfilled. He was driven away from people and ate grass like cattle. His body was drenched with the dew of heaven until his hair grew like the feathers of an eagle and his nails like the claws of a bird (vv. 31-33).

God did this to bring Nebuchadnezzar to his senses. Later when the king looked back on his experience as a wild beast, he realized that his was a case of temporary insanity. "At the end of that time, I, Nebuchadnezzar, raised my eyes toward heaven, and my sanity was restored" (v. 34). A human being has to be out of his mind to glory in himself. The truth is that our accomplishments are minor, our stature is small, and our existence is brief.

I was reminded of this during the summer of 1998 when Mark McGwire of the St. Louis Cardinals set the all-time single season record for home runs. I watched on television as McGwire hit the homer that tied the record formerly held by Roger Maris. As the announcers were marveling at how far he could hit the ball, the producer switched to the television camera in the blimp high above the city of St. Louis. From that vantage point, one could see how small McGwire's accomplishment really was. He was hitting a tiny ball out of a tiny stadium in a tiny spot on the face of a tiny globe in a vast universe. It was all a matter of perspective. Things look different from a blimp than they do from home plate.

To see how small human beings are and how short our existence is, we must look at things from the proper point of view. It was not until Nebuchadnezzar lifted his eyes up to God that he regained his sanity. As long as he was looking at himself, he seemed enormous, and there was no room for God at all. But once he looked to God, he shrank back down to his proper size.

Once he came to his senses, two things impressed Nebuchadnezzar about God. One, of course, was God's sovereignty:

> *All the peoples of the earth*
> *are regarded as nothing.*
> *He does as he pleases*
> *with the powers of heaven*
> *and the peoples of the earth.*
> *No one can hold back his hand*
> *or say to him: "What have you done?"* (v. 35)

Nebuchadnezzar finally learned who was really in charge of the universe: the King of kings. There was something else that impressed the king, too, and that was God's eternity. This was the first thing he mentioned: "Then I praised the Most High; I honored and glorified him who lives forever. His dominion is an eternal dominion; his kingdom endures from generation to generation" (v. 34b).

The braggart of Babylon learned how limited his monarchy was. True, he was the most powerful man in the world, but God could take that power away at any moment, as he had already demonstrated. Nebuchadnezzar's kingdom would not last forever. He himself would die, and his kingdom would pass into the hands of someone else. Eventually, the whole Babylonian Empire would lie buried in the sand.

Contrast that with the kingdom of the everlasting God. Because he lives forever, he will reign forever. His dominion is eternal, and his kingdom is everlasting. He alone is the king eternal, so to him alone belong the kingdom, the power, and the glory forever.

THE ETERNAL SON

The boastful king of Babylon finally learned to worship the King Eternal. But he was not the only one. The prophet Daniel learned the same lesson just a few years later. He had a dream in which he saw four beasts. This is how he described it:

> *In my vision at night I looked, and there before me was one like a son of man, coming with the clouds of heaven. He approached the Ancient of Days and was led into his presence. He was given authority, glory and sovereign power; all peoples, nations and men of every language worshiped him. His dominion is an everlasting dominion that will not pass away, and his kingdom is one that will never be destroyed.* (Dan. 7:13-14)

Daniel used the same vocabulary Nebuchadnezzar used to describe God's everlasting dominion. But his vision also contained something new. In addition to God the Father—called "the Ancient of Days" to emphasize his eternity—Daniel saw "one like a son of man." In other words, he saw someone in the appearance of a human being.

The description of this "son of man" is striking. He comes with the glory-clouds of heaven. He is given sovereign power. He is worshiped by all peoples and nations. And his kingdom is forever. In other words, this son of man possesses the very attributes of God. Although he is a human being, he shares in the glory, sovereignty, and eternity of Almighty God. Who can this be? It is obvious that Daniel was given a vision of the Christ who is both God and man.

Daniel 7 is the passage Jesus had in mind at his trial when the High Priest asked him if he was "'the Christ, the Son of the Blessed One?' 'I am,' said Jesus. 'And you will see the Son of Man sitting at the right hand of the Mighty One and coming on the clouds of heaven'" (Mark 14:61b-62). Jesus identified himself with the Son of Man prophesied in Daniel. He claimed to be equal to the Father in glory, sovereignty, and eternity.

And so he is. Jesus Christ is the Alpha and the Omega, the First and the Last (Rev. 1:8, 17). "He was with God in the beginning" (John 1:2). And he *was* God! God the Son shared in the glory of God the Father even before the world began (John 17:5). "He is before all things" (Col. 1:17). He existed from eternity past in all the glory of his deity. Christ's eternity proves Christ's deity.

When Jesus died on the cross to save us from our sins, it seemed as if his life had come to an end. He was removed from the cross, wrapped in linen, and buried in a tomb for three days. But the eternity of his divine nature did not allow him to remain in the grave. He was brought back to life, and now he will never die again. He will live forever (Heb. 7:24). "Jesus Christ is the same yesterday and today and forever" (Heb. 13:8).

The same may be said of the Holy Spirit. Jesus promised to send a Counselor who would remain with his disciples forever (John 14:16). Thus the Holy Spirit is called "the eternal Spirit" (Heb. 9:14). The divine attribute of eternity belongs to the Father, and to the Son, and to the Holy Spirit, forever.

WHEN TIME SHALL BE NO MORE

All the divine attributes have practical implications for daily life. The eternity of God is no exception.

First, because God is eternal, he is able to threaten eternal damnation. If God did not live forever, then his judgment could not last forever. The curses of Scripture would be nothing more than idle threats. But God will live forever. Therefore, his threatenings of everlasting woe must be taken with complete seriousness.

The person who had more to say about hell than anyone else in Scripture was Jesus Christ. Jesus promised that when he comes in all his glory, he will gather every human being who has ever lived before his throne for judgment. There he will pronounce this sentence upon those who neither loved him nor served him: "'Depart from me, you who are cursed, into the eternal fire prepared for the devil and his angels'" (Matt. 25:41). "'Then they will go away to eternal punishment'" (v. 46), where "the smoke of their torment rises for ever and ever" (Rev. 14:11a).

The reality of eternal judgment depends on the eternity of God. The Puritan Thomas Watson said, "As long as God is eternal, he lives to be avenged upon the wicked. Oh eternity! eternity! who can fathom it? Mariners have their plummets to measure the depths of the sea; but what line or plummet shall we use to fathom the depth of eternity?"[8]

And who, one might add, is able to endure even the thought of being separated from God's love for all eternity? The only sensible thing to do is come to him through Jesus Christ while there is still time.

Second, it is because of his eternity that God is able to guarantee eternal life. The same Christ who threatens the wicked with eternal punishment promises the righteous eternal life (Matt. 26:46). Everyone who believes in the eternal Christ will receive eternal life.

Again and again, especially in the Gospel of John, Jesus gives the free invitation to receive eternal life. He told Nicodemus that "'everyone who believes in him may have eternal life. For God so loved the world that he gave his one and only Son, that whoever believes in him shall not perish but have eternal life'" (John 3:15-16).

The reason Jesus offered eternal life so freely was because he knew he could back up his promise. He knew that since he himself is eternal, he could grant eternal life to everyone who believes in him. "God has given us eternal life, and this life is in his Son" (1 John 5:11).

Obviously, the fact that life in Christ is called "eternal life" says something about how long it will last. In this life we never seem to have enough time, and we never seem to run out of troubles. But in the life eternal all troubles will come to an end, and there will be time to spare. We will live forever in the full joy of God's presence.

The eternity of God is essential to the happiness of heaven. The Puritans liked to say that it is eternity that makes heaven to be heaven. If there were any doubts about God's eternity, then heaven would be full of anxious thoughts. "When will it all end?" the saints would ask. "How much longer do you think God is going to last?"

The truth is that God will last forever. We could no more lose eternal life than God could cease to exist (Hab. 1:12). For that very reason, God's praise will never come to an end. Ever. God's praise, like God himself, is everlasting. His name will be praised forever and forever (Ps. 44:8), for "to him belongs eternal praise" (Ps. 111:10).

The everlasting worship of God is described in the wonderful verse that was later added to John Newton's hymn "Amazing Grace" (1790):

> *When we've been there ten thousand years,*
> *Bright shining as the sun,*
> *We've no less days to sing God's praise*
> *Than when we'd first begun.*

In heaven we will sing God's praise for days without end.

When I was a little boy, I had anxious thoughts about the eternity of God. The last verse of "Amazing Grace" was one of the reasons why. I would lie awake in bed at night and imagine what it would be like to live forever and forever and forever. Then I would start to think about God the Father, God the Son, and God the Spirit existing from eternity past. Then I would run to find my parents. It was too overwhelming to even contemplate.

It still is. The eternity of God is a mystery far beyond the mortal mind. But it is not beyond our worship. We worship God for what we do not understand as well as for what we do understand. However little we may comprehend it, we worship God for his eternal being.

Glory be to the Father, and to the Son, and to the Holy Ghost; as it was in the beginning, is now, and ever shall be, world without end. Amen.

CHAPTER 5

GOD DOES NOT CHANGE

The Story of Saul's Rejection as King

— ∞ —

I the Lord do not change.
So you, O descendants of Jacob, are not destroyed.

MALACHI 3:6

My favorite diner is closed. For years it stood on the same corner, just a few doors down from Rittenhouse Square in
Philadelphia. It always had the same staff, the same menu, the
same decor, even the same customers. Then the diner was
bought out and shut down.

That kind of change happens every day. Business changes—
one shop closes, another shop moves its location, and the build-
ing left behind is abandoned. Fashions change as fads come and
go. The weather changes, sometimes more than once a day.

People change, too. They change jobs. They change
churches. On occasion they change in completely unexpected
ways. You think you know them well, but then all of a sudden
they do something uncharacteristic. People change their looks,
their moods, their habits, even their worldviews.

The more things change . . . the more things change. From
one day to the next, the whole world is a little bit different. The
ancient Greek philosopher Heraclitus (fifth century B.C.)
claimed it was impossible to step into the same stream twice. His
point was that by the time you climb up on the bank and step

back into the stream again, it is no longer the same stream. Its ripples, eddies, and currents have changed. Life is an endless stream of constant flux.

NO SHADOW OF TURNING

There is only One who does not change. The God of heaven and earth is like a granite boulder in the middle of the rapids. While all around is swirling change, he is unchanged and unchanging. And unlike the boulder in the rapids, God does not erode. "Trust in the LORD forever, for the LORD, the LORD, is the Rock eternal" (Isa. 26:4).

Even when there is change all around him, there is no change in God. He is, as the theologians say, immutable. This word comes from the Latin *mutare*, meaning "to change." It forms the basis for the English words *mutation* and *mutant*. A mutant is a creature who has undergone an abnormal change in its appearance. But God is not a creature; he is the Creator. Thus he is immutable. He lives forever without mutation, alteration, variation, or fluctuation. He always remains the same.

The reason God does not change is because he is perfect just the way he is. In his little book on the attributes of God, A. W. Pink writes, "He cannot change for the better, for He is already perfect; and being perfect, He cannot change for the worse. Altogether unaffected by anything outside Himself, improvement or deterioration is impossible. He is perpetually the same."[1]

The immutability of God is different from his eternity, although the two are closely related. In the last chapter we said that God exists from everlasting to everlasting. Here we discover that he is not only eternal, but he is eternally the same. God is exactly the same God he has always been. James Montgomery Boice writes, "The unchangeableness of God (immutability) means that God is always the same in his eternal being."[2] God cannot be otherwise than he is.

Nothing can be added to God—or subtracted from him. He is incapable of augmentation or diminishment. He cannot suffer loss or decay. He is incorruptible, which is what the New Testament means when it says that God is *immortal* (Rom. 1:23; 1 Tim. 1:17).

The Bible uses several pictures to describe the unchangeability of God. The psalmist compares the universe to a set of old, worn-out clothes.

> *In the beginning you laid the foundations of the earth,*
> *and the heavens are the work of your hands.*
> *They will perish, but you remain;*
> *they will all wear out like a garment.*
> *Like clothing you will change them*
> *and they will be discarded.*
> *But you remain the same,*
> *and your years will never end.* (Ps. 102:25-27)

Eventually, the whole universe will need a change of clothes. God will roll up the heavens and the earth and put them out with the trash. But God himself never becomes threadbare. He will remain "brand-new" forever.

The apostle James draws a different picture. His image of God's immutability is a chiaroscuro—a study in light and shadow. "Every good and perfect gift is from above," writes James, "coming down from the Father of the heavenly lights, who does not change like shifting shadows" (James 1:17).

God is the Father of the heavenly lights. He made the sun, the moon, and the stars. All those heavenly bodies are subject to change. They change their positions and vary in their brightness. The planets wander about the heavens. The moon waxes and wanes in its various phases. The sun may be covered by clouds; it shines by day but not in the darkness.

Unlike the heavenly lights, God himself does not change. He is not variable. His attributes do not have a dimmer switch. His glory is never eclipsed or overshadowed. God always shines with the intense brilliance of the noonday sun that streams down and leaves no shadow. In his comments on this verse, Arthur John Gossip invites us to

> . . . think of the glory of a midsummer day, in that hushed hour of noon when everything is still, and the sun blazes down in its meridian splendor until every nook and cranny lies saturated and soaked through and through with warmth and light. Ah! but the sun dips, and the shadows lengthen, and the chill of evening comes, and then the dark. But God's love is a sun that never sets. It is always, always, at its full noonday glory![3]

With God there is no shadow of turning.

What does it mean to say that God is immutable? Following the logic of the Shorter Catechism, it means that he is "unchangeable in his being, wisdom, power, holiness, justice, goodness, and truth."

God's essence does not change. He cannot alter who he is in himself. Human beings have their good days and their bad days. "He's not quite himself today," we sometimes say. But the living God never has an "off-day." His nature and his being are constant.

God's attributes do not change. He is always all-powerful, all-knowing, and all-loving. He is never unjust, unholy, or untrue. As the Puritan Stephen Charnock explained, "God always is what he was, and always will be what he is."[4]

The fact that God is immutable does not mean that he is immobile. Although his attributes do not change, God is active in possessing and exercising them. He always acts in a way that is consistent with himself.

To say that God is immutable also means that his will does

not change. He never changes his mind. He never has a change of heart. And unlike us, he never changes his plans. "The plans of the LORD stand firm forever, the purposes of his heart through all generations" (Ps. 33:11). The reason our plans often change is because we are influenced by our circumstances. We never know for sure what will happen. Life never turns out quite the way we expect, and we have to change our plans accordingly.

God, on the other hand, cannot be influenced by circumstance. He never has an emergency. He never makes a bad choice. "Oops!" is not part of God's vocabulary. Because of his eternal decree and infinite knowledge, things always turn out the way he expects.

God is unchangeable in his being, nature, essence, attributes, and purpose. In the words of Thomas Boston, "He is the same in all his perfections, constant in his intentions, steady to his purpose, unchangeably fixed and persevering in all his decrees and resolutions."[5]

CAN GOD REPENT?

It is at this very point—the divine attribute of immutability—where the biblical doctrine of God is increasingly under attack. A new kind of theology has arisen in recent years, first in Germany, then in Britain, and now in America. Although it started in the universities and secular divinity schools, it is fast becoming part of mainstream evangelical theology.

The new theology has produced a new god, as new theology always does. He is a god who is in process. He does not have an eternal, unchangeable being; he is always becoming something new. Apparently, one must stay tuned for further developments! Over the course of human history, God grows and matures until he reaches his full potential. He is a spontaneous, risk-taking god. He does not know what the future holds because the future partly depends on us. This is all part of what some theologians are calling "the openness of God."[6] Their god is open to possibilities, open to the future, even open to change.

One of the reasons some theologians think God is open to change is because the Bible occasionally says that he "repents." There is an example of this in the story we studied in chapter 3, the story of Jonah. When God saw that the Ninevites were sorry for their sins, "he had compassion and did not bring upon them the destruction he had threatened" (Jonah 3:10). To say that God "had compassion" is literally to say that he "repented."

There are other examples of divine repentance in the Old Testament. God repented that he brought the children of Israel out of Egypt (Ex. 32:14). He even repented that he had created mankind in the first place (Gen. 6:6). These examples raise an important question: If the Bible teaches that God can and does repent, then doesn't that mean that he can change? At the very least, doesn't he change his mind?

The first thing to realize is that when the Bible speaks of God "repenting," it is speaking in human terms. God often stoops down to our level like this. But just because he explains himself in a way we can understand does not mean that he shares our limitations. For example, when the Bible says that God has a mighty arm (e.g., Deut. 7:19), it does not mean that he has a bicep. The Bible speaks truthfully, but not always literally.

Consider another example. Psalm 78:65 says, "Then the Lord awoke as from sleep, as a man wakes from the stupor of wine." But God does not need an alarm clock, for the psalms also say that "he who watches over you will not slumber; indeed, he who watches over Israel will neither slumber nor sleep" (121:3b-4). The reality is that the living God never goes to sleep. When the Bible describes him as "waking up" to do something, it is using a human experience to describe something that goes beyond human experience.

The same is true when the Bible speaks of divine repentance.

God does not repent the way we repent. Of course not. He never makes any mistakes. Therefore, unlike us, he cannot be sorry for what he has done.

When God "repents," so to speak, the change is not in him; it is in our relationship to him. There are changes in us and in God's dealings with us, but not in God himself. The Bible puts this in human terms by saying that God "repents." Yet there is no actual change in God himself. God "may will a change," wrote Thomas Watson, "without changing his will."[7]

God's will does not change. His ways do not change. His nature does not change. His attributes do not change. His eternal purpose does not change. Not even God's mind changes, although it may seem that way to us. As Balaam said to Balak: "God is not a man, that he should lie, nor a son of man, that he should change his mind" (Num. 23:19a).

Often when God seems to change his mind, he is operating according to his covenant. Remember that the covenant God makes with his people has conditions. If you do this, God will do that. Obedience leads to blessing; disobedience leads to judgment. But even when we disobey, there is always the possibility of repentance. With repentance comes forgiveness, and sometimes the removal of God's judgment.

These covenant conditions explain why God sometimes seems to repent. On many of the occasions when God seems to change his mind, what has really happened is that his people have changed their hearts. God explained this to the prophet Jeremiah when he made a visit to the potter's house:

> *"If at any time I announce that a nation or kingdom is to be uprooted, torn down and destroyed, and if that nation I warned repents of its evil, then I will relent and not inflict on it the disaster I had planned. And if at another time I announce that a nation or kingdom is to be built up and planted, and if*

it does evil in my sight and does not obey me, then I will recon-
sider the good I had intended to do for it." (Jer. 18:7-10)

Therefore, even when God "changes his mind," as it seems
to us, he operates according to his eternal plan, what the writer
to the Hebrews calls "the unchanging nature of his purpose"
(6:17). The give and take of our relationship with God is part of
his unchangeable purpose. When the Bible says God "repents,"
it means that "he relents or changes his dealings with men
according to his sovereign purposes."[8]

THOU CHANGEST NOT

There is a story in the Bible about the immutability of God. It is
the tragic story of Saul's rejection as king.

Saul was the first king of Israel. He was anointed by God
through the prophet Samuel. For a time he ruled in strength and
gained victory over his enemies. But then he made a fatal mistake.

What happened was this: God said to Saul, "'Now go, attack
the Amalekites and totally destroy everything that belongs to
them. Do not spare them; put to death men and women, children and infants, cattle and sheep, camels and donkeys'" (1 Sam.
15:3). This was Holy War. Since the Amalekites were the sworn
enemies of God, they deserved to be totally destroyed, along
with everything they owned.

Saul started to carry out God's judgment against the
Amalekites; only he did not get very far.

> *He took Agag king of the Amalekites alive, and all his peo-*
> *ple he totally destroyed with the sword. But Saul and the*
> *army spared Agag and the best of the sheep and cattle, the*
> *fat calves and lambs—everything that was good. These they*
> *were unwilling to destroy completely, but everything that*
> *was despised and weak they totally destroyed.* (vv. 8-9)

In other words, Saul failed to fully carry out God's orders. He spared the best of the livestock for personal gain.

God saw what Saul had done and sent his prophet Samuel to investigate. "When Samuel reached him, Saul said, 'The LORD bless you! I have carried out the LORD's instructions'" (v. 13). But in the background—please feel free to add your own sound effects—Samuel could hear the sound of sheep and cattle. "But Samuel said, 'What then is this bleating of sheep in my ears? What is this lowing of cattle that I hear?'" (v. 14). Baaaa! Moooo!

Saul was caught in the act. He proceeded to do what people usually do in that situation: He tried to rationalize his behavior. "Saul answered, 'The soldiers brought them from the Amalekites; they spared the best of the sheep and cattle to sacrifice to the LORD your God, but we totally destroyed the rest'" (v. 15). First Saul tried to pin the blame on his soldiers. Then he claimed that what he did right made up for what he did wrong.

Samuel wouldn't hear a word of it. Instead, he demanded a full explanation: "'Why did you not obey the LORD? Why did you pounce on the plunder and do evil in the eyes of the LORD?'" (v. 19).

Saul trotted out the same lame excuses again. "'But I did obey the LORD,' Saul said. 'I went on the mission the LORD assigned me. I completely destroyed the Amalekites and brought back Agag their king. The soldiers took sheep and cattle from the plunder, the best of what was devoted to God, in order to sacrifice them to the LORD your God at Gilgal'" (vv. 20-21). Once again Saul blamed his men and came up with a dubious explanation for his actions.

There are many practical lessons to be learned from Saul's misbehavior. The folly of making up your own rules instead of following God's instructions, for example. Or the futility of blaming someone else for your sins. But the main lesson for our purposes is that God does not change.

Samuel pronounced divine judgment against Saul: "'Because

you have rejected the word of the LORD, he has rejected you as king'" (v. 23b). This terrible prophecy filled the king with fear. He even tried to repent for his sins. "Then Saul said to Samuel, 'I have sinned. I violated the LORD's command and your instructions. I was afraid of the people and so I gave in to them. Now I beg you, forgive my sin and come back with me, so that I may worship the LORD'" (vv. 24-25).

Samuel refused to go with Saul, perhaps because this could have been misinterpreted as a sign of God's forgiveness. Whatever the reason, Samuel's refusal made Saul rather desperate, but not so much to have his sins forgiven as to escape his punishment. Scripture paints the pathetic picture of Israel's king grabbing the prophet's robe to prevent him from leaving. While Saul was still holding on to Samuel's robe, the prophet said, "'He who is the Glory of Israel does not lie or change his mind; for he is not a man, that he should change his mind'" (v. 29).

What Samuel said to Saul is a powerful statement of the unchangeability of God. What makes it strange is that it seems that God *has* changed his mind. The same God who anointed Saul to be king has now rejected him. Isn't that a change of plans? In verse 11, God says, "'I am grieved that I have made Saul king.'" Literally, "I repent that I have made Saul king." The same expression is used at the end of the chapter. "The LORD was grieved that he had made Saul king over Israel" (v. 35b).

How do these verses fit together? How can God change his mind in the very same chapter where the Bible says he cannot change his mind?

Scripture itself provides the answer. Notice the reason for God's apparent change of plans: "'I am grieved that I have made Saul king, because he has turned away from me and has not carried out my instructions'" (v. 11). The change was not in God in the first place, but in Saul. This is precisely what we have been saying about divine repentance. The change in Saul leads to the change in God's dealings with Saul. From a human point of view, God has "repented"; yet there is no change in God's eternal plan for a king.

Notice also what Samuel says to Saul in verse 29: "'He who is the Glory of Israel does not lie or change his mind; for he is not a man, that he should change his mind.'" The biblical writer is aware that there is an apparent contradiction in his story, so he adds a clarification. Whatever the Bible means when it says that God "is grieved," or "relents," or even "repents," it is only speaking in human terms. Samuel is careful to make this clear. God is not to be confused with a human being. The reason he never lies or changes his mind is because he is God.

If God were a man, then he could change his mind. He could be persuaded, manipulated, or even bribed. His decrees of judgment could be repealed. But God does not change. He does not say one thing and then do another. It is the very "Godness" of God to remain the same.

J. I. Packer offers this helpful summary of what the Bible teaches—and does not teach—about divine repentance:

> It is true that there is a group of texts which speak of God as repenting. The reference in each case is to a reversal of God's previous treatment of particular men, consequent upon their reaction to that treatment. But there is no suggestion that this reaction was not foreseen, or that it took God by surprise, and was not provided for in His eternal plan. No change in His eternal purpose is implied when he begins to deal with a man in a new way.[9]

God never did change his mind about Saul. He rejected him as king and eventually gave the kingdom to his chosen servant David. Frankly, David turned out to be something of a disappointment as well. He went through some changes of his own, as people often do. But in all of this, God was preparing the way for the King who would not change.

The name of that king is Jesus Christ. In his humanity, of

course, Jesus did change. The Scripture says that as a child he "grew and became strong; he was filled with wisdom, and the grace of God was upon him" (Luke 2:40). In his humanity Jesus even suffered and died for sins.

Yet with respect to his divine nature Jesus is immutable. His deity was not changed by his humanity. His divine being will not change for all eternity. He not only lives forever; he remains the same forever. "Jesus Christ is the same yesterday and today and forever" (Heb. 13:8).

THY COMPASSIONS, THEY FAIL NOT

The unchangeability of God filled Saul with fear. For the Christian, however, there is deep comfort in the fact that God does not change.

In the first place, the immutability of God gives us the confidence to pray. This may seem a surprising thing to say. Often people say just the opposite. "If God has already made up his mind, then why should I pray?" The fact that God does not change seems to make prayer unnecessary.

This is a misunderstanding of both God and prayer. We do not pray in order to change God's mind. I suspect that people who think this way have never seriously considered the alternative. Think for a moment how undesirable it would be to pray to a changeable God.

For one thing, even if you could change the mind of Almighty God, would you really want to? You would be asking for your will to be done rather than for his will to be done. But this is the God who made the world and everything in it. He knows everything about you, down to the very hairs of your head. He is the God who in all things "works for the good of those who love him, who have been called according to his purpose" (Rom. 8:28). Do you *really* want to change his mind?

Prayer is not about us getting our way in heaven; it is about

God doing his will on earth. As we pray, our desires are conformed to the will of the one "who works out everything in conformity with the purpose of his will" (Eph. 1:11). The only proper way to pray is the way our Lord Jesus taught us to pray: "'Your kingdom come, your will be done on earth as it is in heaven'" (Matt. 6:10).

For another thing, if God were changeable, then you could never count on his answers to your prayers. He would not know what the future holds any more than you do. From time to time, you might be able to persuade God to change his mind, but then he could always change it back again. Such a God would be like a weak king, always influenced by the latest advice.

In order for prayer to have any efficacy at all, God must not change. Rather than making prayer unnecessary, the immutability of God is what makes prayer even possible.

Prayer is not the only thing that depends on the fact that God does not change. Our salvation depends on it as well. The immutability of God is the guarantee of our salvation.

Here is a good verse for anyone who doubts the practicality of studying God's attributes: "'I the LORD do not change. So you, O descendants of Jacob, are not destroyed'" (Mal. 3:6). How is that for practical theology? Indeed, what could be more practical? Whether or not you ever draw another breath depends on the immutability of God.

What Malachi means is that if we served a changeable God, he would have gotten rid of us all long ago. We are faithless, hopeless, and loveless. Because we are such flagrant sinners, we deserve to be destroyed. Yet God does not change. His "gifts and his call are irrevocable" (Rom. 11:29). He will never go back on his promise to save us through Jesus Christ. Therefore, the divine attribute of immutability is the guarantee of our salvation.

From time to time most Christians have doubts about themselves. But we never need to have any doubts about God. A. W. Tozer writes:

What peace it brings to the Christian's heart to realize that our heavenly Father never differs from himself. In coming to him at any time we need not wonder whether we shall find him in a receptive mood. He is always receptive to misery and need, as well as to love and faith. He does not keep office hours nor set aside periods when he will see no one. Neither does he change his mind about anything. Today, this moment, he feels toward his creatures, toward babies, toward the sick, the fallen, the sinful, exactly as he did when he sent his only-begotten Son into the world to die for mankind. God never changes his moods or cools off in his affections or loses his enthusiasm.[10]

A. W. Pink makes much the same point:

Herein is solid comfort. Human nature cannot be relied upon; but God can! However unstable I may be, however fickle my friends may prove, God changes not. If He varied as we do, if He willed one thing today and another tomorrow, if He were controlled by caprice, who could confide in Him? But, all praise to His glorious name, He is ever the same. His purpose is fixed, His will is stable, His word is sure. Here then is a rock on which we may fix our feet, while the mighty torrent is sweeping away everything around us.[11]

Through all the changes of life, God never changes. Ultimately, our salvation depends on his unchanged, unchanging, unchangeable love.

This was Oliver Cromwell's (1599-1658) comfort at the very end of his life. Although he tried to serve God as the army general and the prime minister of Puritan England, Cromwell committed many sins, and he knew it. He died on a wild autumn day when the winds were howling, and his soul passed through dark despair.

As death approached, Cromwell spoke to his minister. "Tell me, is it possible to fall from grace?"

"No, it is not possible," answered the minister.

"Then I am safe," said the dying man, "for I know that I was once in grace." Cromwell thought about this for a while longer, and then he said, "I think I am the poorest wretch that lives, but I love God; or rather, am beloved of God."[12]

This is the assurance of every Christian in life and in death. You are beloved of God. His love for you will never, ever, ever fail, because God does not change.

CHAPTER 6

THE GREAT I AM

The Story of Moses and the Burning Bush

———— ∞∞∞ ————

And without faith it is impossible to please God,
because anyone who comes to him must believe that he exists
and that he rewards those who earnestly seek him.

HEBREWS 11:6

"Is God Dead?" That was the startling question raised by the
stark, black cover of *Time* magazine in April of 1966.

The question was first raised back in the nineteenth century
by Friedrich Nietzsche (1844-1900), who said, "If there is a
God, how can I bear not to be God?" Nietzsche decided that he
could not bear it, so he tried to do away with God altogether,
triumphantly announcing God's demise.

This theme was echoed in a poem by the English writer
W. H. Auden (1907-1973):

> *Let aeroplanes circle moaning overhead*
> *Scribbling on the sky the message He Is Dead.*[1]

By the 1960s Nietzsche's ideas had made their way into the
seminaries, where they produced what was called "The Death of
God Theology." Scholars were writing books with titles such as
The Gospel of Christian Atheism and *Theology After the Death
of God* (even though a theology without a God is an inherent
contradiction). One scholar even wrote God's epitaph: "God is

dead, thank God!"² What these so-called theologians were saying ᵗwas that when Jesus of Nazareth died on the cross, God died
with him. Thus the death of God was a historical event.
Eventually even the most outrageous ideas make their way
from the classroom to the newsstand. Hence the question on the
cover of *Time*: "Is God Dead?"

The same question might well be asked today, for practical
atheism has become one of the major religions of postmodern
times. To be a practical atheist is to live as if God did not exist.
Even many people who claim to be religious live as if they did
not believe in God at all. They leave God out of their work, their
entertainment, their daily conversation, and their plans. To
them—for all practical purposes—God is dead.

ARGUMENTS FOR GOD'S EXISTENCE

The truth is that God remains very much alive and well. Our
study of his attributes brings us to the very fact of his being.

The case for God's existence is often made by argument.
Some of the arguments are good ones. The first is the argument
from reality. Why is there something rather than nothing?
Where do time and space and matter come from? Why is there
a physical universe at all?

These are questions that cannot be answered without a
God. The theory of evolution cannot answer them. Whatever
else it may be, evolution is *not* a theory of origins. It is a theory of changes. It tries to explain how one creature evolved
into another. But it cannot explain why there should be any
creatures in the first place. Or why there should be anything
at all, for that matter. Evolutionary theory has never offered
an explanation for the origin of life. Even if it could, it has no
explanation for the existence of the conditions that led up to
the origin of life.

Evolutionism is like the ancient fable that the world rests on the back of a giant turtle. The story is told of a skeptic who wanted to find out if this was true. He went to a guru and said, "Tell me, is it true that the earth rests on the back of a giant turtle?"

"Yes," said the guru, "it is as you say."

"But what holds up the turtle?" the skeptic demanded.

"Why, another turtle, of course."

"And what is beneath that turtle?" the skeptic wanted to know. "Surely not another turtle!"

By this point the guru was starting to become exasperated, so he said, "Look, it's turtles all the way down!"

A similar sort of argument is often made about the universe. One thing came from another thing, which came from something else. But you are still left with this question: Why is there anything at all? Evolutionism is a "turtles-all-the-way-down" kind of explanation. It does not explain where the turtles came from in the first place. Even if you go all the way back to the first moments of the universe, you still need to know who put the boom into the Big Bang.

The most plausible explanation for the existence of everything rather than nothing is God. Nothing comes from nothing. Nothing ever could. Matter is not eternal. It does not cause itself to exist. By definition, there is only one being who is timeless and transcendent. The Bible teaches that he is the one who made the world and everything in it out of nothing. "In the beginning God created the heavens and the earth" (Gen. 1:1). God is "the alone fountain of all being, of whom, through whom, and to whom, are all things."[3]

A second argument for the existence of God is the argument from design, which takes the argument from reality one step further. Not only does the universe exist, but it is so beautiful and perfect in its construction that it must have a maker. Its design gives evidence of its designer.

Everywhere we look in the universe, we see the fingerprints

of Almighty God. "The heavens declare the glory of God; the skies proclaim the work of his hands" (Ps. 19:1).

Consider the laws of the physical universe. Scientists have shown that there are at least twenty-five constants necessary for the existence of life.[4] In order for life to be possible these constants must be precisely what they are. So, for example, if the strong nuclear force were any stronger than it is, it would be impossible for hydrogen to form; if it were any weaker, hydrogen would be the only element in the universe. Either way, life would be impossible.

Another example is the rate of the universe's expansion. If it expanded any more rapidly than it does, then stars, galaxies, and planets would never form. If it expanded any less rapidly, the whole universe would collapse upon itself. Here is the awesome fact: In order for our universe to exist, its rate of expansion must be accurate to one part in 10^{57}. As your local mathematician can tell you, that is a number vast beyond comprehension. Yet this number is only one of at least twenty-five constants necessary for the possibility of life.

Or consider the behavior of the electron. The 1998 Nobel Prize for physics was awarded to three Americans who discovered the "fractional quantum Hall effect." This discovery changed the way scientists view the interactions among electricity, magnetism, and matter. The prize-winners showed that when electrons are squeezed between two layers of semiconductor material and subjected to a strong magnetic field, they act in concert, behaving like a single particle. This completely unexpected result raises an important question: Who is the designer who coordinated the motions of the electrons?

Everything in the universe—from the smallest subatomic particle to the most distant galaxy—gives evidence of intelligent design. The more we know about the physical universe, the more certain the existence of God becomes, even to secular scientists. The popular British astrophysicist Paul Davies, for example, used to be an atheist. God has since changed his mind. Davies now believes there is "powerful evidence that there is something going behind it all. . . . It seems as though somebody has fine-tuned nature's numbers to make the Universe. . . . The impression of design is overwhelming."[5]

Even scientists who are hostile to the Christian faith are struggling against the reality of design. When I was a student at Oxford, the famous evolutionary biologist Richard Dawkins was a vocal opponent of Christianity, arguing that the study of theology had no place in a modern university. This is how he begins his book *The Blind Watchmaker*: "Biology is the study of complicated things that give the appearance of having been designed for a purpose." Dawkins recognizes that the universe appears to have been designed, yet he proceeds to argue that it was not designed after all! It simply gives "the illusion of design and planning."[6]

Francis Crick, the brilliant scientist who won the Nobel Prize for discovering the structure of DNA, keeps running into the same difficulty. He writes, "Biologists must constantly keep in mind that what they see was not designed, but rather evolved."[7] Apparently, it is not easy to be a biologist and an atheist at the same time. You really have to be careful in the laboratory. You keep finding evidence of design all over the place, so you have to keep reminding yourself that the universe is not designed.

The truth is that even a bucket of pond scum provides incontrovertible evidence of intelligent design. One does not have to be a scientist to know this. Even a glimpse of the first colors of autumn on the far hills reveals the work of the great Artist. "For since the creation of the world God's invisible qualities—his eternal power and divine nature—have been clearly seen, being understood from what has been made, so that men are without excuse" (Rom. 1:20). Wherever we find intricate and beautiful design, we know there is a designer.[8]

The designer has a name. He is called God, and he made every-thing there is just the way it is.

A third argument for the existence of God is the argument from morality. If there is no God, then there can be no objec-tive moral values. In the absence of God, morality becomes a matter of personal preference. Your values are just your opinion.

Moral relativism has become one of the popular ideas of postmodern times. But it leaves a person without any ability to discern the difference between right and wrong. When someone does something morally wrong, all you can say is, "I don't like that." The Christian apologist Ravi Zacharias has a clever response for someone who claims that morals are relative. He asks, "Some cultures love their neighbors, while other cultures eat them . . . which do you prefer?"

Morality is more than a preference. Some things are wrong no matter how many people say they are right—genocide, for example, or child abuse, or murdering a homosexual. Such actions are wrong, and they always will be wrong, whether soci-ety will say so or not. There is an objective difference between right and wrong.

The existence of right and wrong explains why every human being has a troubled conscience. Why is it that human beings feel guilty about some of their actions, even if they think that morals are relative? The Bible gives the reason. It teaches that the requirements of God's law are written on every human heart (Rom. 2:15). Part of the evidence for God's moral law is a per-son's own guilty conscience.

If it is true that there are objective moral values, then it fol-lows that there must be a moral law. But if there is a moral law, then there must be a moral lawgiver, and we have reasoned our way back to God. We live in a moral universe because it is God's universe.

THE REAL PROOF

The three arguments we have made for God's existence—from reality, from design, and from morality—show how plausible it is to believe that there is a God who made and rules the universe. But they are not proofs.

Somewhat surprisingly, the Bible never sets out to prove the existence of God. Instead, it treats his existence as self-evident. God is not someone to be proved; he is someone to be assumed. In order to make sense of anything at all you have to begin with God. His existence is so obvious that the Swiss theologian Francis Turretin (1623-1687) called it the "indubitable first principle of religion."[9]

God is the starting point for all human thought. You cannot even argue that God does not exist without employing the reason God has infused into the universe. Nor can you shake your fist at God without using a fist God designed in the first place.

Perhaps an example will help. Suppose you reject God because there is so much evil in the world. There *is* great evil in the world, and Christians have to live with it, wrestle with it, and try to explain it like everyone else. But does the presence of evil disprove the existence of God?

If you believe that there is such a thing as evil, then you must believe that there is such a thing as good. There has to be a standard of comparison. Evil is only known to be evil by the presence of good. But then there must be a standard for determining the difference between good and evil. If there is a standard, then there must be a standard-giver, and you have reasoned your way right back to God again.

This is why the Bible says, concerning anyone who tries to deny God's existence, "The fool says in his heart, 'There is no God'" (Ps. 14:1a). Whether or not it can be proven, God's existence is so obvious that you would have to be a fool not to believe it. If you do not believe in God, you are in a weak position intellectually. The great preponderance of the evidence is against you, as is the great majority of human opinion, not to mention your own conscience. Is it possible that by rejecting God you are making a giant fool out of yourself?

GOD IS WHO HE IS

I hope you are convinced that God exists. That is a good first step. However, God wants more from you than a grudging acknowledgment that he exists. He wants you to know him in a personal way. There is a story about this in the Bible, the story of Moses and the burning bush.

Moses believed in the existence of God (Heb. 11:24-28). He was a Hebrew by birth, and all the Hebrews believed in God. But when Moses saw an Egyptian beating a Hebrew slave, he murdered the Egyptian and buried him in the sand.

Although Moses was careful not to let anyone see what he had done, the word got out. Pharaoh himself heard about the homicide and signed the death warrant. So Moses became a fugitive from justice. He fled Egypt and went to live in Midian, where he found work as a shepherd, saying, "'I have become an alien in a foreign land'" (Ex. 2:22).

One day while Moses was tending his flock, he saw a strange sight near Horeb, the mountain of God. "There the angel of the LORD appeared to him in flames of fire from within a bush. Moses saw that though the bush was on fire it did not burn up" (3:2). This was so unusual that he went over to investigate. How could the fire continue to burn without consuming the bush?

When Moses got closer, he was personally confronted with the God who exists. "When the LORD saw that he had gone over to look, God called to him from within the bush, 'Moses! Moses!'" (v. 4).

The Bible does not say how close Moses was to the bush, but however close it was, it was close enough!

"Do not come any closer," God said. "Take off your sandals, for the place where you are standing is holy ground." Then he said, "I am the God of your father, the God of Abraham, the God of Isaac and the God of Jacob." At this, Moses hid his face, because he was afraid to look at God. (vv. 5-6)

It is one thing to believe in the existence of God, as Moses always had. But it is something else to come into God's very presence and to meet him in all his holiness.

God had pity on Moses and spoke kind words to him. God had seen the misery of his people in captivity. He had heard their prayers. He was concerned about their suffering. He had come to rescue them and to give them a good land. He was also putting Moses in charge, with the guarantee that he would go with him.

All of that was good news, but Moses was still worried. Put yourself in his bare feet for a moment. He could hardly believe his own eyes, let alone convince anyone else of what he had seen. He also knew how skeptical people would be. He could imagine himself going back to Egypt and saying, "Look, I was out in the desert watching these sheep, and there was this bush, see, and it kept on burning without burning up. Anyway, then I heard a voice telling me to lead you out of Egypt."

It was not hard to guess what people would say about that! They would say that Moses had been seeing things and hearing things. Then how should he respond—"I guess you had to be there"? Moses needed some proof. So he asked for better credentials. "Moses said to God, 'Suppose I go to the Israelites and say to them, "The God of your fathers has sent me to you," and they ask me, "What is his name?" Then what shall I tell them?'" (v. 13).

Moses already knew he was in the presence of the God of Abraham, Isaac, and Jacob. But by asking for the divine name, Moses was asking God to tell him exactly who he was.

The answer God gave is a great statement of the reality of his being:

> *"I AM WHO I AM. This is what you are to say to the Israelites: 'I AM has sent me to you.'"*
>
> *God also said to Moses, "Say to the Israelites, 'The LORD, the God of your fathers—the God of Abraham, the God of Isaac and the God of Jacob—has sent me to you.' This is my name forever, the name by which I am to be remembered from generation to generation." (Ex. 3:14-15)*

God's special name has never been forgotten. To give but one example, it is incorporated in the seal of certain French Protestant groups. Their insignia depicts a burning bush imprinted with the Hebrew letters for the divine name: "YHWH."

For the Jews those letters are forever sacred. According to some, although God's name may be written—it appears more than 5,000 times in the Old Testament—it is blasphemy to speak it. Perhaps that is why the proper pronunciation for God's name, which was well known in biblical times, has long since been forgotten. The King James Version of the Bible sometimes writes it out as "Jehovah." The *New International Version* simply prints it as "LORD" in small capital letters. Probably the way to say God's special name was something like "Yahweh."

WHAT'S IN THE NAME?

If you want someone to know who you are, the first step is to give your name. God has given us his name so we may know him. But what does his name *mean*?

First, *Yahweh* means that God is mysterious. By giving us his name, God lets us know who he is. But God's name itself shows that there are some things about him we will never know. The great Dutch theologian Herman Bavinck (1854-1921) wrote, "God *is* that which he *calls* himself, and he *calls* himself that which he *is*."[10] So who is God? God is who he is. Any more questions?

Second, God's name means that he is eternal and unchangeable (or immutable). His special name shows that he possesses the attributes described in the previous two chapters. His name is the present tense of the Hebrew verb "to be." God does not say, "I was who I was," or "I will be who I will be." He says, "I am who I am." That is because he has no past or future, only an eternal present. God is who he is; he has always been who he is; and he always will be who he is.

God's name has a third meaning. It means that he is self-existent. Everything else owes its being to God, but God is independent. He does not owe his being or his attributes to anyone else. He simply exists all by himself. As the Puritan Matthew Henry (1662-1714) observed, "The greatest and best man in the world must say, By the grace of God *I am what I am;* but God says absolutely—and it is more than any creature, man or angel, can say—*I am that I am.*"[11]

For several years now I have been collecting theological questions I have been asked by my children. Together they form what I call the "Parents' Catechism." As catechisms go, this one is pretty tough. Most of the questions are impossible to answer, even if one holds a doctorate in historical theology. The first question is this: "Who made God?"

The answer, of course, is that no one made God. He simply is who he is in himself. Theologians sometimes call this the *aseity* of God. The word *aseity* is derived from the Latin *a,* meaning "from," and *se,* meaning "himself." God has his existence "from himself." He is not dependent on anyone or anything else.

Everything we have said about God's special name so far is summarized by J. I. Packer: "This 'name' is not a description of God, but simply a declaration of His self-existence, and His eternal changelessness; a reminder to mankind that He has life in Himself, and that what He is now, He is eternally."[12]

Another way to say this is that God is self-sufficient. He does not have any unmet needs or unsatisfied desires. He does not need any help. He is not codependent. He is not living on bor-rowed time. He does not live or move or have his being in any-one except himself.

This idea of self-sufficiency, too, was part of the meaning of the burning bush. Before God *told* Moses who he was, he *showed* him who he was. The striking thing about the burning bush was that the fire did not depend on the bush for fuel. It just kept burning and burning all by itself. Similarly, God does not get his energy from anyone or anything else. The burning bush symbolizes his eternal and self-existent being. To quote again from the Westminster Confession of Faith, "God hath all life, glory, goodness, blessedness, in and of himself; and is alone in and unto himself all-sufficient, not standing in need of any crea-tures which he hath made."[13]

The attributes represented by God's name are amazing enough. But here is the truly amazing thing: God is who he is for the salvation of his people. When Moses went back to his people, he did not simply tell them, "I have seen the great I AM." Instead, his message was that the great I AM had seen them and was about to save them! The eternal, unchangeable, self-existent God of all the universe knew and cared about their sufferings and would go with them to save them from their enemies.

This point needs to be applied in a personal way. The God who is there is there for you. He has seen your misery. He knows your suffering, and he cares for you. He has heard your prayers. He will rescue you and bring you to a good and perfect place. God is who he is for your salvation.

When we discover that God is not simply somewhere out there, but here, for us, we can only follow the example of Moses. When he met the great I AM at the burning bush in all the full-ness of God's mysterious, eternal, and unchangeable being, Moses knew he was standing on holy, holy, holy ground. He took off his sandals, hid his face, and worshiped God. Whenever we worship, we enter the presence of the same great I AM, who is too holy for our shoes. We can only bow down and worship.

JESUS IS THE GREAT I AM

Perhaps you accept God's existence in a general sort of way, but have never come to him in a relationship of trust and friendship. If that is the case, then realize that the Bible says that "without faith it is impossible to please God, because anyone who comes to him must believe that he exists and that he rewards those who earnestly seek him" (Heb. 11:6).

Two things are necessary. First, you must believe that God exists, which you would have to be a fool not to believe. Second, you must seek after God. God wants you to seek him so that you come to know him in a personal way. The only way to know God in this personal way is to know him through Jesus Christ.

Jesus of Nazareth went around making audacious claims about himself. Many of them began with the words God spoke to Moses: "I am." Jesus was forever saying "I am" this and "I am" that. "'I am the bread of life'" (John 6:48). "'I am the good shepherd'" (10:11). "'I am the resurrection and the life'" (11:25). "'I am the way and the truth and the life'" (14:6).

On several occasions, Jesus said the most remarkable thing of all. He simply said, "I am." Once he was talking to some religious leaders at the temple in Jerusalem. He said in a sort of off-hand way, "'Abraham rejoiced at the thought of seeing my day'" (8:56). It was an outrageous thing to say. Who did Jesus think he was, claiming to know what was on Abraham's mind? Abraham had been dead for 2,000 years! "'You are not yet fifty years old,' the Jews said to him, 'and you have seen Abraham!'" (v. 57).

Then Jesus said something even more outrageous. "'I tell you the truth,' Jesus answered, 'before Abraham was born, I am!' At this, they picked up stones to stone him" (vv. 58-59a). Skeptics sometimes say that Jesus never claimed to be God. But the Jews who were with him that day knew better. They understood exactly what Jesus was saying, which is why they tried to stone him for blasphemy. Jesus was putting himself on equal terms with Almighty God. He was claiming to be the great I AM, the eternal and self-existent God incarnate.

Jesus made the same claim the night before he died on the cross for sins. He had been praying with his disciples in the Garden of Gethsemane. Suddenly Judas came to betray him, followed by an unholy alliance of priests and soldiers.

Jesus stepped forward and said, "'Who is it you want?'" (John 18:4). When they told him that they were looking for Jesus of Nazareth, he had just two words (in the original Greek) for them: "'I am'" (v. 5). When Jesus spoke those words, the priests and the soldiers fell to the ground. They responded this way for the same reason Moses hid his face: They had come face to face with the great I AM.

Did you know that Jesus was present at the burning bush? This important detail is sometimes overlooked. Moses saw a being in the burning bush, apparently in human form. The Bible says that "the angel of the LORD appeared to him in flames of fire from within a bush" (Ex. 3:2). The most probable explanation is that Moses saw the eternal Son of God in his preincarnate form. No angel would have accepted Moses' worship, let alone demanded it, as this "angel" did. Therefore, we may conclude that Jesus was the great I AM at the burning bush, as he is now and ever shall be.

Have you met the great I AM the way Moses did? The only way to know God in a personal way is to come to him through Jesus Christ. Jesus said, "'If you do not believe that I am, you will indeed die in your sins'" (John 8:24). If you want to be saved from sin, death, and the meaninglessness of life, it is not enough to believe in the mere existence of God. You must believe in Jesus Christ, for he is the great I AM.

CHAPTER 7

GOD HAS ALL THE ANSWERS

The Story of Job and the Tempest

—∞∞—

Oh, the depth of the riches of the wisdom and knowledge of God!
How unsearchable his judgments, and his paths beyond tracing out!
"Who has known the mind of the Lord? Or who has been his counselor?"

ROMANS 11:33-34

It is not easy to know what God is doing. It is hard to tell, for example, what he is doing in history. Every week there is news of a natural disaster, a tragic accident, a financial crisis, or an armed conflict somewhere in the world. It is often hard to make sense of global events.

Nor is it easy to know what God is doing in your own life. A prayer goes unanswered. A longing remains unsatisfied. Something precious is taken away. So it is hard to know what on earth God is doing, either in the world at large or in the world as you know it.

The English poet William Cowper (1731-1800) sometimes struggled to understand what God was doing in his life. Cowper battled severe depression, and during one of his down times he wrote:

> *God moves in a mysterious way*
> *his wonders to perform;*
> *He plants his footsteps in the sea,*
> *and rides upon the storm.*

Cowper borrowed his striking image from the Psalms: "Your path led through the sea, your way through the mighty waters, though your footprints were not seen" (Ps. 77:19). It is the biblical way of saying that God does not leave any tracks. He works in the world like he is walking across the stormy seas. But if the only footprints he leaves behind are in the ocean, how can anyone know where he has been, where he is going, or what he is doing?

GOD ONLY WISE

The only thing we know for sure is that whatever God is doing is wise. We know this, not from experience, primarily, but because the Bible tells us that wisdom is one of the divine attributes.

Wisdom is closely related to knowledge. God is as infinite in knowledge as he is in everything else. He is "omniscient," as the theologians say, or all-knowing. "The LORD is a God who knows" (1 Sam. 2:3). He knows "the thoughts of man" (Ps. 94:11). He knows "the secrets of the heart" (Ps. 44:21; Acts 15:8). He knows his sheep (John 10:14). He knows you by name (Jer. 1:5), and he knows what you need (Matt. 6:8). God knows everything in the universe in precise detail, down to the last sparrow (Matt. 10:29).

Has it ever occurred to you that nothing ever occurs to God? God knows all things, including the future. His knowledge is partly foreknowledge. He knows the end from the beginning (Isa. 46:10). He never learns from history, and he never hears any news. God remembers everything that has happened in the past, he is familiar with everything that is happening at this very moment, and he is already aware of everything that will happen in days to come. His exhaustive knowledge of the past, present, and future extends throughout the whole universe.

A. W. Pink summarizes the knowledge of God by saying, "God is omniscient. He knows everything: everything possible, everything actual; all events, all creatures, of the past, the present and the future. He is perfectly acquainted with every detail in the life of every being in heaven, in earth and in hell."[1]

The word the Westminster Shorter Catechism uses to describe God's intellect is not knowledge, however, but wisdom. Wisdom is a kind of knowledge, only more practical. With God it is applied omniscience. According to Herman Bavinck, it involves "choosing the best end and the best means for reaching that end."[2]

Wisdom requires discernment and good judgment. Knowledge has the facts, but it takes wisdom to know what to do with them. It is one thing to know the difference between latitude and longitude; it is another thing to find your way out of the woods using a map and a compass. Knowledge is the kind of thing they teach at school; wisdom is a skill that is learned from life experience.

The mind of God contains all the treasures of both wisdom and knowledge (Rom. 11:33). He is the "only wise God" (16:27). Sinclair Ferguson explains what this means:

> The wise man is the one who sees his goal, recognises the best ways to achieve that goal, and then implements those ways. The wisdom of God is similar: God puts his glorious purposes into effect in order to demonstrate his perfect knowledge, sovereign power, and infinite grace. God's wisdom is evident as he takes the raw, fallen materials of this world and its history to weave a garment of praise and glory for his name.[3]

When the Bible speaks of God's wisdom, it gives two main examples: creation and redemption. God is wise both in the way he made the world (creation) and in the way he saves his people (redemption).

Divine wisdom is displayed, first of all, in creation. There is wisdom in the way God made the earth, the sky, and the sea.

By wisdom the LORD laid the earth's foundations,
by understanding he set the heavens in place;
by his knowledge the deeps were divided,
and the clouds let drop the dew. (Prov. 3:19-20)

God made the earth by his power;
he founded the world by his wisdom
and stretched out the heavens
by his understanding. (Jer. 10:12)

There is wisdom, too, in the way God made the animals. After praising the beasts of the field, the birds of the air, the donkeys, the cattle, the storks, and the lions, the psalmist exclaims, "How many are your works, O LORD! In wisdom you made them all; the earth is full of your creatures" (Ps. 104:24).

In the words of the famous children's hymn by Cecil Frances Alexander (1823-1895), "*All things bright and beautiful / all creatures great and small / all things wise and wonderful / the Lord God made them all.*" That is the wisdom of creation.

God's wisdom is also displayed in the redemption of lost sinners through the death and resurrection of Jesus Christ. "In him we have redemption through his blood, the forgiveness of sins, in accordance with the riches of God's grace that he lavished on us with all wisdom and understanding" (Eph. 1:7-8). From beginning to end, the whole plan of salvation shows infinite wisdom.

Anselm of Canterbury (1033-1109) raised a famous question about salvation. He posed it to God himself: "How dost Thou spare the wicked if Thou art just, supremely just?"[4] Anselm found his answer in divine wisdom.

Many years later the Scottish theologian Thomas Boston told a story to explain what Anselm discovered about God's wisdom. Boston began by defining the problem. God is just, so he must punish our sins. It would be unjust for him to do otherwise. But God is also merciful, so he wants to pardon our sins. So Boston imagined the attributes of God holding an argument in heaven about the fate of humanity. Justice demanded that sinners be punished, while Mercy begged for their pardon. How could both of these divine attributes be satisfied?

Then Wisdom stepped forward to provide the solution, which Boston described as follows:

> When man had ruined himself by sin, all the wisdom of men and angels could never have devised a method for his recovery. Heaven seemed to be divided upon this awful event. Mercy inclined to save man, but Justice interposed for satisfaction. . . . In this hard exigence the wisdom of God interposed, and in the vast treasure of its incomprehensible light, found out an admirable expedient to save man without prejudice to the other divine perfections. The pleas of Justice, said the wisdom of God, shall be satisfied in punishing, and the requests of Mercy shall be granted in pardoning. . . . I will have an infinite sacrifice to content Justice, and the virtue and fruit of that sacrifice shall delight Mercy. . . . My Son shall die, and satisfy Justice by his death; and by the virtue and merit of that sacrifice sinners shall be received into favour, and herein Mercy shall triumph and be glorified. Here was the most glorious display of wisdom.[5]

The cross of Christ is a just mercy and a merciful justice. This is its wisdom (1 Cor. 1:24). The crucifixion harmonized the mercy and the justice of God. Having paid the price owed to justice, Jesus Christ now offers mercy as a free gift. His cross makes God both "just and the one who justifies those who have faith in Jesus" (Rom. 3:26), and thereby preserves the integrity of God's attributes. Without question, it took infinite wisdom to make mercy and justice embrace in this way.

THE SUFFERINGS OF JOB

We know that God is wise. We can see his wisdom in creation and redemption. But we do have a problem, and it lies at the personal level. When it comes to our own circumstances, we sometimes wonder whether God is very wise after all. There seems to be a gap between our theology and our reality.

Thankfully, there is a Bible story to help us understand God's wisdom in our sufferings. It is the story of Job and the tempest.

Job was one of God's favorite people. He was the wealthiest and most famous man in the Middle East at that time. He was so godly that God himself used him as the prime example of a righteous man. "'Have you considered my servant Job?'" God asked. "'There is no one on earth like him; he is blameless and upright, a man who fears God and shuns evil'" (Job 1:8; 2:3a).

There was no one on earth like Job, but no one has ever suffered the way he suffered either. In short order he lost his oxen, his donkeys, his sheep, and his camels. His servants were slain by enemies. All his sons and daughters were killed by a tornado. Then he was afflicted with painful sores from the bottom of his feet to the top of his head. After this onslaught, Job tore his robe, shaved his head, sat down among the ashes, and scraped himself with a piece of broken pottery. The man went from the top of the world to the top of the garbage dump.

Apart from his wife, the only thing Job had left in the world were a few friends. At first they were very sympathetic to his plight. As soon as they heard what happened to Job, they left their homes to look for him. When they found him, they hardly recognized him, so great was his suffering. Because they loved the man, they wept aloud, tore their robes, and sprinkled dust on their heads. "Then they sat on the ground with him for seven days and seven nights. No one said a word to him, because they saw how great his suffering was" (2:13).

Job had good friends. Unfortunately, they eventually found their tongues. When they did, what they had to say was not very comforting. They wanted to explain to him "'what wise men have declared'" (15:18), which was exactly the problem: They offered conventional wisdom rather than God's wisdom.

The doctrinally correct view in those days was that a man's suffering was the result of his own sin. If Job was suffering, well, then it was obvious that God was judging him for his sins. It was as simple as that. Job's trials were Job's fault. All he needed to do was repent for his sins, and then everything would be fine.

The counsel Job received from his friends was clear, it was doctrinal, it was practical, but it was wrong. Although Job's friends knew a little theology, they did not know how to apply it to his case. In other words, they knew just enough doctrine to be dangerous.

Just about the last thing Job needed was someone to straighten out his theology. He already believed in the only wise God. He accepted wisdom as one of the divine attributes. We know this because Job often mentions it. "'The fear of the Lord—that is wisdom, and to shun evil is understanding'" (28:28). The wisdom of God was the starting point for Job's doctrine of God.

Job had seen the wisdom of God in creation. He said, "'His wisdom is profound, his power is vast'" (9:4a). Then he recounted God's mighty acts in earth and heaven:

> "He shakes the earth from its place
> and makes its pillars tremble.
> He speaks to the sun and it does not shine;
> he seals off the light of the stars.
> He alone stretches out the heavens
> and treads on the waves of the sea.
> He is the Maker of the Bear and Orion,
> the Pleiades and the constellations
> of the south." (9:6-9)

Not only had Job seen the wisdom of God in creation, but he also knew that God was wise in redemption. "By his power he churned up the sea; by his wisdom he cut Rahab to pieces" (26:12). He knew God had both the wisdom and the power to save his people from their enemies, here represented by the sea monster Rahab.

In chapter 28 Job goes on a quest to find wisdom. "'Where can wisdom be found?'" he asks (v. 12a). He tries to beg, borrow, or buy it wherever he can. But wisdom cannot be found among men. It does not live at the bottom of the sea. It cannot be purchased with gold or silver. Its price is beyond rubies.

"'Where then does wisdom come from?'" Job asks again (28:20a). Here is the end of his quest:

> "God understands the way to it
> and he alone knows where it dwells,
> for he views the ends of the earth
> and sees everything under the heavens.
> When he established the force of the wind
> and measured out the waters,
> when he made a decree for the rain
> and a path for the thunderstorm,
> then he looked at wisdom and appraised it;
> he confirmed it and tested it." (28:23-27)

Even in his grief and suffering, Job remained absolutely convinced that "'to God belong wisdom and power; counsel and understanding are his'" (12:13). That is why God himself approves of Job's theology at the end of his book, telling Job's friends, "'You have not spoken of me what is right, as my servant Job has'" (42:7).

In short, whatever else Job may have needed from his friends, he did not need a new theology. In his excellent book on suffering, Dan McCartney points out that Job had an existential problem, not a doctrinal problem. "In fact, Job's existential problem presupposes the doctrine. If he did not believe in a just and sovereign God, he would have no grounds for questioning God."[6] It was exactly because Job believed in God's wisdom that he failed to understand what God was doing in his life.

The longer Job suffered, the more questions he had. By the

middle of the book, he starts to confront God. He wants to sit God down and get some answers out of him.

> *"If only I knew where to find him;*
> *if only I could go to his dwelling!*
> *I would state my case before him*
> *and fill my mouth with arguments.*
> *I would find out what he would answer me,*
> *and consider what he would say." (23:3-5)*

People often find themselves in Job's position. We encounter trials and hardships. We pray for them to go away. Sometimes they do not go away. We do not then cease to believe in God's existence or stop trusting in him. In a way, we still believe in his wisdom. But we do want to sit God down and get some answers.

C. S. Lewis described this attitude in a famous essay called "God in the Dock." The "dock" is the box in the English courtroom where an accused criminal sits. That is exactly where the modern skeptic wants to put God. Lewis writes:

> The ancient man approached God as the accused person approaches his judge. For the modern man the roles are reversed. He is the judge: God is in the dock. He is quite a kindly judge: if God should have a reasonable defence for being the god who permits war, poverty and disease, he is ready to listen to it. The trial may even end in God's acquittal. But the important thing is that Man is on the Bench and God in the Dock.[7]

Thus man claims the right to interrogate God and sit in judgment over him.

JOB IN THE DOCK

Eventually Job did get his day in court. It did not turn out quite the way he expected, however. For one thing, the meeting did not take place in court after all. The Lord God of Israel—the same "Yahweh" who spoke to Moses from the burning bush— spoke to Job out of a tempest. For another thing, God never answered any of Job's questions.

The Bible says, of course, that "the LORD answered Job out of the storm" (38:1). But what kind of answer did he give? God's "answer" began with another question! "'Who is this that darkens my counsel with words without knowledge?'" (v. 2). This was God's way of telling Job, "Don't ask that question!"

God then proceeded to ask Job question after question after question—sixty-four questions in all, depending on how one counts. They are questions to stagger the mind and amaze the intellect.

> "Where were you when I laid the earth's foundation?
>   Tell me, if you understand." (v. 4)
> "Who shut up the sea behind doors
>   when it burst forth from the womb . . .
> when I said, 'This far you may come and no farther;
>   here is where your proud waves halt'?" (vv. 8, 11)
> "Have you ever given orders to the morning,
>   or shown the dawn its place?" (v. 12)
> "Have you entered the storehouses of the snow
>   or seen the storehouses of the hail,
> which I reserve for times of trouble,
>   for days of war and battle?" (vv. 22-23)
> "Can you bind the beautiful Pleiades?
>   Can you loose the cords of Orion?
> Can you bring forth the constellations in their seasons
>   or lead out the Bear with its cubs?" (vv. 31-32)
> "Do you give the horse his strength
>   or clothe his neck with a flowing mane?" (39:19)
> "Does the hawk take flight by your wisdom
>   and spread his wings toward the south?" (v. 26)

Good questions. By posing them, God was reminding Job of the wisdom of his creation. Even Job's own wisdom, such as it was, came from God, for "'Who endowed the heart with wisdom or gave understanding to the mind?'" (38:36).

If only God is so wise, then what right does Job have to question his judgment?

> *"Will the one who contends with the Almighty correct him?*
>   *Let him who accuses God answer him!"* (40:2)
> *"Would you discredit my justice?*
>   *Would you condemn me to justify yourself?*
> *Do you have an arm like God's,*
>   *and can your voice thunder like his?*
> *Then adorn yourself with glory and splendor,*
>   *and clothe yourself in honor and majesty.* . . . .
> *Then I myself will admit to you*
>   *that your own right hand can save you."* (40:8-10, 14)

Job knew there was nothing he could say to all that, so he did not even try:

> *"I am unworthy—how can I reply to you?*
>   *I put my hand over my mouth.*
> *I spoke once, but I have no answer—*
>   *twice, but I will say no more."* (40:4-5)

God put Job back in the dock, where he belonged. The dock is where human beings always belong, as Eugene Peterson explains in his commentary on Jeremiah:

> We think that God is an object about which we have questions. We are curious about God. We make inquiries about God. We read books about God. We get into late night bull sessions about God. We drop into church from time to time to see what is going on with God. We indulge in an occasional sunset or symphony to cultivate a feeling of reverence for God.

But that is not the reality of our lives with God. Long before we ever got around to asking questions about God, God has been questioning us. Long before we got interested in the subject of God, God subjected us to the most intensive and searching knowledge.[8]

If anyone is going to the ask the questions, it is going to be the God who knows all the answers. By interrogating Job, God reclaimed his right to do the asking.

LIVING WITHOUT ALL THE ANSWERS

What do we learn about suffering from God's questions? First, that we should not expect God to give us all the answers.

To be sure, God could have explained himself to Job. He could have explained why he allowed Job to suffer poverty, grief, and illness. But then he would have been giving Job the right to question his judgment. That is not the way the universe works. We do not sit in judgment over God; God sits in judgment over us. There are times when he keeps the wisdom of his counsel to himself.

Even sound theology does not give us all the answers. It reveals the character of God and the plan of salvation, but it does not explain what God is doing in a particular life at a particular moment. We do not know the details of God's plans. They are not recorded in Scripture or revealed by special inspiration. God's purposes for us are known only to him.

The case of Job is a good example. The opening chapters of the book of Job show that God did not cause Job's suffering. Satan was the one who came and tormented Job (1:6-12; 2:1-7). God allowed this in order to gain victory over Satan, but he did not cause it. Job did not suffer because he needed to be punished, but because God would be glorified through his obedience.

But Job never knew any of that, at least in this life. He never learned that his suffering was a sign of God's favor. He never figured out that he suffered, not because he was unrighteous, but because he was righteous. God knew the answers, of course, but he kept them to himself.

When it comes to suffering, God usually keeps the answers to himself. Why does he allow you to suffer? Ultimately, all suffering is the result of his curse against human sin (see Gen. 3:15). But there are many reasons why God may allow his children to suffer in a particular circumstance.

Sometimes Christians suffer in order to know the sufferings of Christ. Suffering is part of what it means to be united to Jesus Christ (Phil. 3:10-11). Sometimes Christians suffer to give a faithful testimony to this lost world or to be trained in righteousness (Heb. 12:7-8). Some lessons can only be learned through suffering. Through suffering Christians are prepared for glory (2 Cor. 4:17).

A Christian may suffer for any and for all of these reasons. But do not expect God to explain himself to you! Often it is part of his wisdom *not* to explain himself. As J. I. Packer says, "the truth is that God in His wisdom, to make and keep us humble and to teach us to walk by faith, has hidden from us almost everything that we should like to know about the providential purposes which He is working out in the churches and in our own lives."[9] In the meantime, all we can do is trust God's wisdom to know what he is doing.

This brings us to a second lesson: The story of Job and the tempest shows that we can live without all the answers.

At first, Job thought he couldn't live without answers. That is why he was sitting out on the garbage dump, feeling sorry for himself. He said, "Listen, God, unless I start getting some answers, I just can't go on."

So God called Job's bluff. He started listing all the things Job accepted even though he could not explain them: The stars in the heavens. The waves on the seashore. The first light of dawn.

The water cycle in the desert. The universe is full of things we cannot control or explain, but simply accept as a matter of course. Why should the ups and downs of life be any different? Living without all the answers is part of what it means to be a human being.

At the end of all his trials, Job decided—answers or no answers—to keep on living. This is what he said to God:

> *"I know that you can do all things;*
> *no plan of yours can be thwarted.*
> *You asked, 'Who is this that obscures my counsel*
> *without knowledge?'*
> *Surely I spoke of things I did not understand,*
> *things too wonderful for me to know.*
> *You said, 'Listen now, and I will speak;*
> *I will question you,*
> *and you shall answer me.'*
> *My ears had heard of you*
> *but now my eyes have seen you.*
> *Therefore I despise myself and repent*
> *in dust and ashes."* (Job 42:2-6)

The argument was over. Job finally gave in to God, not because he was able to prove God wrong, or because he understood why bad things happen to good people, but because he decided to trust God's wisdom. He had always believed that God was wise, but now he understood what it meant to entrust his life to that wisdom.

Job's faith is an example for everyone who is still looking for some answers. If God has enough wisdom to manage the boundaries of the sea, the motions of the heavens, and the instincts of the animals, he has more than enough wisdom to run your life. To quote again from Thomas Boston, "To this wise God we may safely entrust all our concerns, knowing he will manage them all so as to promote his own glory and our real good."[10]

This brings us to another lesson: God knows all the answers. Just because God does not always give us the answers does not mean that there aren't any. The Bible says that "all the treasures of wisdom and knowledge" are hidden in Jesus Christ (Col. 2:3). Jesus is "wisdom from God" (1 Cor. 1:30).

Even Job was looking forward to the day when God would give us wisdom incarnate. He said, "'I know that my Redeemer lives, and that in the end he will stand upon the earth'" (Job 19:25). The name of that Redeemer, although Job did not know it at the time, is Jesus Christ.

When Jesus came to earth, in all his wisdom, he did not give us a philosophic answer to our sufferings. Instead, he entered right into our sufferings, even to the point of death. By dying on the cross, Jesus provided God's ultimate answer to the problem of human suffering. On the cross he paid for the sins that cause suffering in the first place. One day soon, by virtue of that death, Jesus will bring all our sufferings to an end, and "there will be no more death or mourning or crying or pain" (Rev. 21:4).

But that time has not yet come. God, in his infinite wisdom, is allowing us to suffer a little while longer. In the meantime, we must trust that the only wise God knows what he is doing.

CHAPTER 8

THE LORD GOD OMNIPOTENT REIGNS

The Story of the Empty Tomb

——∽∽∽——

His incomparably great power for us who believe . . . is like the working
of his mighty strength, which he exerted in Christ when he raised him
from the dead and seated him at his right hand in the heavenly realms,
far above all rule and authority, power and dominion, and every title
that can be given, not only in the present age but also in the one to come.

EPHESIANS 1:19B-21

I remember standing near the banks of the Chesapeake on a
warm November night, listening to the beautiful strains of
Mozart's Piano Concerto #20. The moon had not yet come up
over the watery horizon, so the night was black. The stars were
bright and shining, and I was gasping for breath, my arms reaching for the heavens, overcome by the power of God.

There were so many stars! I thought of Abraham standing in
the desert under the black skies of Mesopotamia, trying to count
them all. God said, "'Look up at the heavens and count the
stars—if indeed you can count them'" (Gen. 15:5). I imagined
Abraham trying to count them: ". . . 162, 163, 16—wait a second now. Did I count that one already or not?" So he would
start all over again: "1, 2, 3, 4 . . ."

Even when he was done counting, Abraham didn't know the
half of it. He did not begin to understand the vast mysteries of

interstellar space. He had not peered through super telescopes at the galaxies in the far reaches of the universe. He did not know that there are billions of stars, in billions of galaxies, billions of light years away, or that it would take him more than a million lifetimes to travel to the nearest star.

But as he looked up into the heavens, Abraham did know this: God spoke the absolute truth when he appeared to him and revealed his name, saying, "'I am God Almighty'" (Gen. 17:1). Only an all-powerful God could make this universe.

HOW GREAT IS GOD ALMIGHTY

God is all-mighty. This is the first article in the Apostles' Creed: "I believe in God the Father Almighty." God, as the Shorter Catechism expresses it, is "infinite, eternal, and unchangeable in his . . . power." His power is total, absolute, and unending. He is omnipotent, meaning "all-powerful." Nothing is too difficult for God (Jer. 32:17). Nothing is impossible for God (Luke 1:37). He can do whatever he likes.

From time to time skeptics have objected to the idea of an omnipotent God. The philosopher Charles Hartshorne, for example, has written a book with the blasphemous title *Omnipotence and Other Theological Mistakes*.[1]

"You say God is omnipotent?" the skeptic asks. "Then answer me this: Can he draw a round square? Can he make a rock so heavy that he can't lift it?" Such questions seem to pose dilemmas. If God is unable to make a rock too heavy to lift, then there is at least one thing he cannot do. But if he could make the rock, he would be unable to lift it, and there still would be at least one thing he could not do. Therefore, the argument goes, there is no all-powerful God.

That kind of reasoning shows the danger of speculating about God without having a relationship with him. Once you come to know the living God the way Moses and Job came to know him, then you stop treating him like an idea. God is not a list of philosophical propositions; he is a personal God.

Because God is personal, all his attributes hold together. To ask if God can do something self-contradictory (like draw a round square) is to separate his power from his logic. But God's power cannot overthrow his reason. Reason, power, and all the rest of the divine attributes belong together in his being. When we say that God is all-powerful, we mean that he can do whatever he wants, in keeping with his wise plan.

The Catechism for Young Children is careful about how it defines God's power. "Can God do all things?" "Yes," goes the answer, "God can do all his holy will." That answer harmonizes God's power with his wisdom. God is able to do whatever he wills. The only things he wills to do are those things that are wise and sensible.

There are some things God cannot do, therefore, as the Bible itself teaches. God cannot lie (Heb. 6:18). He cannot change his mind (Num. 23:19) or his character (James 1:17), as we were reminded back in chapter 5. He cannot sin (James 1:13). He cannot deny himself (2 Tim. 2:13). God cannot do any of these things because he would have to un-God himself to do them. Nevertheless, he is omnipotent, meaning that he can do all his holy will.

The Puritan Stephen Charnock explained God's power in plain seventeenth-century English: "The power of God is that ability and strength whereby He can bring to pass whatsoever He pleases, whatsoever His infinite wisdom may direct, and whatsoever the infinite purity of His will may resolve."[2] God's unlimited power is directed by his pleasure, wisdom, and will.

The Bible gives many examples of God's potency, but they fall into two main categories: creation and salvation. God has revealed his power, first by making the world (creation) and then by rescuing it (salvation).

First, creation. "God made the earth by his power" (Jer.

10:12a). Everything he has made—from the smallest quark to the brightest quasar—is a testimony to his mighty strength. The starry autumn sky is an excellent example:

> *Lift your eyes and look to the heavens:*
> *Who created all these?*
> *He who brings out the starry host one by one,*
> *and calls them each by name.*
> *Because of his great power and mighty strength,*
> *not one of them is missing.* (Isa. 40:26)

God's power is demonstrated not only by what he has made, but also by the way he made it. God made everything out of nothing by the word of his power. He is so amazingly powerful that all he had to do was say the word, and it was so.

Listen to the rhythm of the creation history. "And God said, 'Let there be light,' and there was light" (Gen. 1:3). "And God said, 'Let the water under the sky be gathered to one place, and let dry ground appear.' And it was so" (v. 9). "And God said, 'Let there be lights in the expanse of the sky. . . .' And it was so" (vv. 14-15).

God said it, and it was so. Thus, when the psalmist praised God for the power of his creation, he wrote,

> *By the word of the* LORD *were the heavens made,*
> *their starry host by the breath of his mouth. . . .*
> *For he spoke, and it came to be;*
> *he commanded, and it stood firm.* (Ps. 33:6, 9)

The omnipotent God created all things by his omnipotent word.

God not only made everything by his word, but he also sustains it by his word. He continues to preserve and provide for his creation, and he does this by his word. At this very moment Jesus Christ is holding the whole world together. He is, the

Scripture says, "sustaining all things by his powerful word" (Heb. 1:3). Thus it is the word of Almighty God that keeps the entire universe from disintegrating into chaos and nothingness.

To praise God for his power is, first of all, to praise him for his work of creation.

> *Each little flow'r that opens,*
> *Each little bird that sings,*
> *He made their glowing colors,*
> *He made their tiny wings. . . .*
>
> *The tall trees in the greenwood,*
> *The meadows where we play,*
> *The flowers by the water*
> *We gather ev'ry day.*
>
> *He gave us eyes to see them,*
> *And lips that we might tell*
> *How great is God Almighty,*
> *Who has made all things well.*

Cecil Frances Alexander taught her Sunday school children to sing those words in 1848. One does not have to be a Sunday school student, however, to recognize God's creative power. One does not even have to be a Christian. God's omnipotence is evident from the very nature of things. "For since the creation of the world God's invisible qualities—his eternal power and divine nature—have been clearly seen, being understood from what has been made, so that men are without excuse" (Rom. 1:20). Power is God's most obvious attribute since it is displayed in everything he has created.

LAZARUS, COME OUT!

A person does have to be a Christian, however, to know God's power in a second way—by salvation. God's creative power is equaled only by "the saving power of his right hand" (Ps. 20:6).

It was by his power that God brought his people Israel out of the land of Egypt, out of the house of bondage. He saved them "with great power and a mighty hand" (Ex. 32:11). It was by his "power and might" that God drove Israel's enemies out of the Promised Land (2 Chron. 20:6-7).

By his power God defended Israel. When Jerusalem was surrounded by Sennacherib and his Assyrian armies, King Hezekiah said, "'Be strong and courageous. Do not be afraid or discouraged because of the king of Assyria and the vast army with him, for there is a greater power with us than with him. With him is only the arm of flesh, but with us is the LORD our God to help us and to fight our battles'" (2 Chron. 32:7-8a). God is omnipotent to save.

If God is going to save us, he must save us from our last enemy—death. There is a story in the Bible about God's power over that enemy. It is the story of the empty tomb.

The first empty tomb in the Gospels was not the tomb of Jesus of Nazareth, but the tomb of Lazarus of Bethany. Lazarus was a close friend of Jesus. He lived not far from Jerusalem with his two sisters, Mary and Martha.

It happened that Lazarus came down with a serious illness. His health declined so rapidly that "the sisters sent word to Jesus, 'Lord, the one you love is sick'" (John 11:3). Mary and Martha knew that Jesus loved their brother. They also knew he was the only one who could save him. But Jesus did not rush to their aid, as they expected. He just dilly-dallied around for a while, or so at least it seemed. Lazarus died before Jesus made it back to Bethany. He was too late to save him.

When Jesus arrived in Bethany, he found the community in mourning. Mary, Martha, and all their loved ones had come face to face with the awful power of death. They were powerless—powerless to heal disease, powerless to preserve life, powerless to conquer death, and powerless to overcome their grief.

We can imagine how they felt, for their impotence is common

to humanity at all times and in all places. Human beings suffer. Human beings get sick and die. Their absence brings the sorrow of loss. Even after all our advances in medical technology, we have not found a cure for the common death.

In their grief, the two sisters both said the same thing to Jesus: "'Lord, if you had been here, my brother would not have died'" (John 11:21, 32). For days, probably, they had been saying it: "If only Jesus had been here." There was more than regret in those words. Mary and Martha reproached Jesus because he had let them down. If he had been there—as he would have been if he had stayed in Bethany, or at least come when they called— Lazarus would still be alive.

What the sisters did not understand was the extent of Jesus' power. They had seen enough miracles to know something of his power, but they did not yet believe that he possesses all power. They believed in his potency, but not his omnipotence. Thus their words placed a limitation on what Jesus could do: "If you had been here." They thought Jesus was limited by time and space, that he had to be with them to help them. They believed in a Jesus who could save them somewhere and sometime, but not right here and right now.

Even Martha, for all her faith, did not fully comprehend Jesus' divine power. She said, "'I know that even now God will give you whatever you ask'" (v. 22). This verse is puzzling. It is not clear what Martha thought Jesus would do, but her "whatever" did not include a resurrection. The thought never entered her mind. We know this because of the way she reacted later at the tomb. When Jesus asked the people to roll away the stone, Martha thought he was out of his mind (v. 39).

It was not that Martha did not believe in the resurrection. She *did* believe. When "Jesus said to her, 'Your brother will rise again,'" she wistfully answered, "'I know he will rise again in the resurrection at the last day'" (vv. 23-24). Martha trusted God to raise his people on the day of judgment.

What Martha did not believe was that God's Son also had omnipotent saving power to raise the dead. She loved Jesus. She worshiped Jesus. She trusted Jesus. She even believed that he was "'the Christ, the Son of God, who was to come into the world'" (John 11:27). But her understanding of Jesus did not yet include the divine attribute of omnipotence.

The same could be said for the rest of the mourners at the tomb of Lazarus. They were as melancholy as Martha. "Some of them said, 'Could not he who opened the eyes of the blind man have kept this man from dying?'" (v. 37). Like Martha, they believed that Jesus had some power, but not all power. They did not understand that he *is* "the power of God" (1 Cor. 1:24).

The reaction of these mourners is understandable because, humanly speaking, their situation was hopeless. Once a man is dead, nothing can be done to save him. And Lazarus was dead. Real dead, as John is careful to show in his Gospel:

> *Jesus, once more deeply moved, came to the tomb. It was a cave with a stone laid across the entrance. "Take away the stone," he said.*
> *"But, Lord," said Martha, the sister of the dead man, "by this time there is a bad odor, for he has been there four days."* (John 11:38-39)

Martha is identified, notice, as "the sister of the dead man." Her brother was so dead that his body had already started to decompose. Death is a nasty, unpleasant business. This is given maximum effect in the King James Version, where Martha says, "'Lord, he stinketh'" (v. 39 KJV).

But Jesus came to overcome death with all its stench. First, he had the people roll away the stone, probably so they could catch a whiff of death for themselves. Then he prayed. When he was finished praying, "Jesus called in a loud voice, 'Lazarus, come out!'" (v. 43). Lazarus came out, still wrapped in white linen. To make sure the eyewitnesses would remember this miracle, Jesus gave them some hands-on experience with it. He said, "'Take off the grave clothes and let him go'" (v. 44).

The Lord Jesus Christ performed this miracle to show that even death is subject to his mighty power. What is most amazing of all is that Jesus performed it simply by his word. He said, "'Lazarus, come out!'" and it was so. The dead man came stumbling out of the tomb to prove that salvation—like creation—comes from the mouth of God. God saves the way he creates—simply by the word of his power.

Many of Christ's divine attributes were displayed in the raising of Lazarus. His fury showed his wrath against the powers of hell (v. 33). His tears showed his compassion for all who suffer (v. 35). The miracle itself showed his love for Lazarus. But what the empty tomb showed most of all was his divine power over death.

In this miracle Jesus was preparing the way for his own death and resurrection. Like Lazarus, he died and was buried in a tomb. Also like Lazarus, he was brought back from the grave. The difference was that when Jesus died, he died to save his people from their sins. Therefore, when he was raised, he gained eternal power over sin and death. "Through the Spirit of holiness [Jesus] was declared with power to be the Son of God by his resurrection from the dead" (Rom. 1:4). The empty tomb is proof for the omnipotence of the triune God.

POWER TO SAVE

The Bible praises the "mighty strength" that God "exerted in Christ when he raised him from the dead and seated him at his right hand in the heavenly realms" (Eph. 1:19-20). It promises that the same "incomparably great power [is at work] for us who believe" (v. 19). How so? How does God put his power to work for us?

First, *God is all-powerful to save you.* The truth is that we cannot save ourselves. We do not love God, cannot obey him, and will not serve him. Until we come to Jesus Christ, we are dead in our sins (Eph. 2:1). Sin is like the toe tag on the body of a fallen soldier. We are not half-dead or mostly dead; we are absolutely dead. If we are to be saved, someone will have to come dig us out of the grave. R. V. G. Tasker describes our plight: "The sin which results in death, from which Jesus by the exercise of His redemptive power raises men to eternal life, is no temporary misfortune, no passing ailment, no sad accident, but a deep-seated malady perpetually corroding and disintegrating human life. It is a 'sickness unto death'."[3]

Dead men cannot raise themselves. That is why Jesus Christ can never be the ultimate self-help program. If we are to be saved at all, God will have to do it for us. All of it. The good news about Jesus Christ is that he "is the power of God for the salvation of everyone who believes" (Rom. 1:16a).

This is the lesson Martha learned. She was hoping God would save her somehow in the end, but Jesus offered her salvation right then and there. "Jesus said to her, 'I am the resurrection and the life. He who believes in me will live, even though he dies; and whoever lives and believes in me will never die. Do you believe this?'" (John 11:25-26).

To know Jesus is to live. It is to have life at this very moment and to keep on having it for all eternity. The same Jesus who has proven his power over death has the power to grant eternal life. He asks us the same question he asked Martha: "Do you believe this?"

Well, do you? Do you believe that Jesus is the Christ, the Messiah God always promised to send? Do you believe he is the Son of God, God as well as man? Do you believe that he is the resurrection and the life, that to believe in him is to escape from eternal death? If you do believe in Jesus, then you will live forever with God, even after you die a physical death.

Martha believed in Jesus, and so did many of her friends.

"Many of the Jews who had come to visit Mary, and had seen what Jesus did, put their faith in him" (John 11:45). For them, seeing was believing. But not everyone believed. "Some of them went to the Pharisees and told them what Jesus had done" (v. 46). Sadly, although they saw Lazarus come back from the grave, they never saw the glory of God. If you want to see the glory of God, you must trust the all-powerful Jesus to save you.

Second, *God is all-powerful to save others*. Once you know the saving power of Jesus Christ, you want everyone else to know it as well. Yet some people seem rather hopeless. They are not interested in Christianity. They are already committed to another religion or to no religion at all. They are so far from God that one wonders how they could ever be saved.

But do not give up hope for them. As soon as you begin to think that anyone is beyond redemption, you have ceased to believe in the God of the Bible, because he is omnipotent. With him all things are possible (Matt. 19:26).

The great missionary Robert Morrison (1782-1834) was a man who believed in God's power to save sinners. His particular ambition was to claim China for Jesus Christ. When he made his first voyage to China, the captain of the ship asked him, "Do you expect to convert China?"

"No," answered Morrison, "but I expect God will."[4]

The power to save sinners comes from God himself. He saves sinners the same way he made the world and the same way he raises the dead—by his word. If we are ineffective in evangelism, it may be because we doubt God's power to save sinners by his word.

Jack Miller wrote a helpful book called *Powerful Evangelism for the Powerless*. He began by asking why the American church has not experienced revival to the same extent in the twentieth century that it did back in the 1800s. Here is Miller's answer:

I am convinced that what gave evangelists in the eighteenth century remarkable power was the Whitefield-Wesley confidence in the supreme authority of Christ. Jesus acted in and through them not because they were powerful persons, but because they were empty vessels needing grace. He was the one who forgave and cleansed them; He was the one who sent them with the gospel; and He was the one who opened the hearts of hardened people to a very humbling message. By contrast, believers today typically serve a much smaller Christ.[5]

It is worth pausing to ask the question: How big is your Christ? Is he the Christ of the empty tomb, who holds all power over sin and death? Is he the Christ of the resurrection, who has the power to bring the dead back to life? If not, then your Christ is too small.

Miller went on to explain the true source of power for evangelism:

The leaders of the Great Awakening had extraordinary power in evangelism and renewal. They followed an omnipotent Christ, the divine warrior, and He anointed them with His missionary presence. But this power was poured out on those who knew that they were inherently powerless without a constant dependence upon the working of God's grace in their lives.[6]

It is doubtful whether we will see very many people saved until we begin to follow the same omnipotent Christ, who is all-powerful to save.

POWER FOR THE POWERLESS

Miller's emphasis on God's power to use weak servants brings us to a third point of application: *God is all-powerful to send you into his service.* Some Christians hold back from serving God—particularly in the area of evangelism—because they are not sure they will be any good at it. But holding back from God's service is really another way of denying his omnipotence.

To believe in God's power is to believe that he can use us to do his work. In fact, it is when we are weakest that God shows himself to be strongest. This is the lesson the apostle Paul learned through his "thorn in the flesh," whatever it may have been (2 Cor. 12:7). Paul wanted to have a powerful ministry. He thought that the stronger he was, the more effective he would be in God's service.

God taught Paul that just the opposite was the case. God wanted his apostle to remain weak in his flesh in order to become strong in his ministry. He said, "'My grace is sufficient for you, for my power is made perfect in weakness'" (v. 9). As long as the power came from Paul himself, it could not come from God. But God brought him to the place where he could say, "'When I am weak, then I am strong'" (v. 10b).

This is the great paradox of Christian life and ministry: God's power flows through our weakness. This is as true for us as it was for our Savior. "He was crucified in weakness, yet he lives by God's power. Likewise, we are weak in him, yet by God's power we will live with him to serve you" (13:4). Rather than asking God to make us strong, therefore, we should ask God to make himself strong through our weakness.

In 1998 Clyde McDowell, the president of Denver Seminary, was diagnosed with a malignant brain tumor, a cancer that eventually claimed his life. Dr. McDowell wrote a circular letter about what it was like to suffer the gradual loss of his powers:

> It is God's will for me to submit to His sovereignty, accept His plan (as unexpected as it may be), and focus simply on a submissive attitude. . . . This relinquishing allows me to be released of the messianic burden I sometimes carry, which is to feel responsible to change the world and fix its problems. . . . As a man of faith and submission to the Lordship

of Christ, I must grow in humility and watch the mighty hand of God accomplish His purpose without the false expectation that God must have my help.

This is what it means to believe in God's omnipotence. It is to trust in his power and not our own.

Finally, *God is all-powerful to solve your problems.* Since I am a minister, people often bring me their problems. Sometimes they try to prove that they are beyond my help. Their marriage is irreconcilable. Their gifts are unusable. Their sin is unpardonable. It almost seems as if they want me to agree that their problems cannot be solved.

In a way, they are right. I cannot solve my own problems, let alone anyone else's. But I refuse to agree that anyone's problems *cannot* be solved. God is too powerful for that. No one is beyond his help. What I try to say to people, as gently as possible, is this: "I don't care what your problem is, God is not overpowered by it."

When it comes to your problems—temptation, loneliness, conflict, illness, poverty, persecution, grief, whatever—God is all-powerful. He may not solve your problems the way you would like him to. Probably he won't, which was one of the lessons Job learned. But God is not overpowered by your problems. Stephen Charnock wrote, "Our evils can never be so great to oppress us as his power is great to deliver us. The same power that brought a world out of chaos, and constituted and hath hitherto preserved the regular motion of the stars, can bring order out of our confusions, and light out of our darkness."[7]

Scripture assures us that God's "divine power has given us everything we need for life and godliness" (2 Peter 1:3). By his power, God will continue to give us everything we need for this life and the life to come. "By his power God raised the Lord from the dead, and he will raise us also" (1 Cor. 6:14; cf. Phil. 3:21).

Once God raises us from the dead, we will praise him for his omnipotence. We will praise him for the power of his creation, using the lyrics printed on the back pages of Scripture:

> *"You are worthy, our Lord and God,*
> *to receive glory and honor and power,*
> *for you created all things,*
> *and by your will they were created*
> *and have their being."* (Rev. 4:11)

And we will praise him for the power of his salvation, which saves us from sin and from every other trouble:

> *"Hallelujah!*
> *Salvation and glory and power*
> *belong to our God. . . .*
> *Hallelujah!*
> *For our Lord God Almighty reigns."* (19:1b, 6b)

CHAPTER 9

HOLY, HOLY, HOLY

The Story of Isaiah at God's Heavenly Throne

———

The Lord is in his holy temple;
let all the earth be silent before him.

HABAKKUK 2:20

People do not talk much about the holiness of God anymore. The subject never comes up in the news. It is not discussed at the corner barber shop. It is not a topic one overhears from a nearby table at the food court. People do not talk about the pure, majestic holiness of God.

People *were* talking about God's holiness back in 739 B.C., however, the year that King Uzziah died. Uzziah had been a good king. He was righteous. The Bible says he "sought God" and "did what was right in the eyes of the LORD" (2 Chron. 26:4-5). He was strong. He conquered the Philistines and rebuilt Jerusalem. His kingdom stretched from Egypt to Syria. "His fame spread far and wide, for he was greatly helped until he became powerful" (v. 15b).

But Uzziah became proud of his accomplishments, and pride led to his downfall. He decided that since he was the king, he could do whatever he pleased. One day he went to the temple and barged into the Holy Place to burn incense on the altar.

When Azariah and the other priests saw what Uzziah was about to do, they followed him into the Holy Place. They found the king with the censer in his hand, ready to burn incense. "They confronted him and said, 'It is not right for you, Uzziah, to burn incense to the LORD. That is for the priests, the descendants of Aaron, who have been consecrated to burn incense. Leave the sanctuary, for you have been unfaithful; and you will not be honored by the LORD God'" (2 Chron. 26:18).

Uzziah was livid. Who did the temple staff think they were, ordering the king around like that? "While he was raging at the priests in their presence before the incense altar in the LORD's temple, leprosy broke out on his forehead" (2 Chron. 26:19b). Immediately, the king was forced to leave the temple because he was unclean. Uzziah remained a leper until the day he died. He had to live in a separate house. He was excluded from God's presence because he had violated God's holiness.

THE KNOWLEDGE OF THE HOLY

Holiness means separation. Something holy is set apart. It is sacred. It is distinguished from what is common or ordinary and dedicated to the Lord.

The Old Testament contains a long list of things that were set apart. The people of Israel were holy. The covenant sign of circumcision separated them from the world. The priests were holy. They were distinguished from the rest of God's people by their sacred calling. The temple was holy. It was consecrated for worship. The Sabbath day was holy because it was different from ordinary weekdays (Ex. 20:11). Even certain kinds of food were holy. God's people made a distinction between the clean and the unclean in their eating habits (Lev. 11:47). Thus they were constantly reminded of the difference between the holy and the unholy.

God's people had to be holy because God himself is holy. "'You are to be holy to me because I, the LORD, am holy, and I have set you apart from the nations to be my own'" (Lev. 20:26). The word

the Bible uses to describe God more than any other word is *holy*.[1]
He is the Holy One, and "knowledge of the Holy One is understanding" (Prov. 9:10b). He is the unique and supreme holiness,
for "there is no one holy like the LORD" (1 Sam. 2:2).

To say that God is holy means more than just that he does
not sin. That is true, of course. God is morally upright. He is
righteous and undefiled. His "eyes are too pure to look on evil"
(Hab. 1:13a). He does not sin; indeed, he cannot. Thus Alec
Motyer defines the holiness of God as "his total and unique
moral majesty."[2]

God's holiness refers to more than his ethics, however.
Holiness is the beauty of God's being and essence. It refers to
everything that distinguishes him from us. It includes his
majesty, purity, otherness, and transcendence. Holiness is the
separation between the Creator and the creature, the infinite distance between God's deity and our humanity. Holiness is the
very "Godness" of the God who says, "'I am God, and not
man—the Holy One among you'" (Hos. 11:9). In response, his
creatures can only say, "Who is like you—majestic in holiness,
awesome in glory, working wonders?" (Ex. 15:11).

God is so holy that everything associated with him is holy.
His name is holy (Ps. 103:1). His Word is holy (2 Tim. 3:15).
His law is holy (Rom. 7:12). His promise is holy (Ps. 105:42).
His works are holy (Ps. 145:17). His ways are holy (Ps. 77:13).
His wrath is holy (Ps. 2:4-6). Even his people—as unholy as we
are—are holy, at least in the sense that we are set apart for his
service (1 Peter 2:9).

One way the holiness of God was expressed in the Old
Testament was in the organization of the temple. The temple
was God's house. It contained the Ark of the Covenant, which
represented God's presence with his people.

At the same time, however, the temple showed the vast distance between God and his people. A series of courtyards, walls,
and veils separated them from his holy presence. First there was

the court of the Gentiles, which was open to people from all nations. A low wall separated the court of the Gentiles from the court of the women. This, in turn, was separated from the court of Israel by a high wall. Next came the court of the priests, which was surrounded by pillars and a railing. Within the court of the priests was the Holy Place, which Uzziah unlawfully entered. It was concealed by a veil of thick cloth. Inside the Holy Place there was another veil to hide the Holy of Holies.

What all these barriers communicated was the holiness of God. They said, "Warning! Keep your distance! The area you are about to enter is holy ground." As people approached God at the temple, they had to go through ceremonial washings and sacrifices to purify themselves.

Only one person went into the Holy of Holies, and only once a year. The High Priest entered on the Day of Atonement. Can you imagine the palpitations of that man's heart as he parted the veil and stepped into the Most Holy Place? He wore little bells around his robe that would jingle as he made atonement for the sins of God's people. He wore them so the other priests would know if he was still alive(!), or if perchance he had been destroyed by the sheer holiness of God.

Not everyone survived an audience with God unscathed. King Uzziah certainly did not. "For years the king had lived in alienation and separation, under divine displeasure, and as his death approached he remained, to the human eye, uncleansed."[3] It was all because Uzziah had dropped in on God uninvited. Even when God is present with his people—as he was at the temple—he remains awesome in his holiness.

IN THE THRONE ROOM OF GOD

Because of Uzziah's experience, godly people were talking about God's holiness in the days of Isaiah. They had a keen sense of God's

majesty, especially when they went to the temple. They probabl.
went around on tiptoe, worshiping with fear and trembling.

Whatever fears Isaiah may have had were realized when he
went to visit God on his holy throne. The story of this encounter
is told in five parts.

1. The first is what the prophet saw: *God reigning.* Isaiah
entered the throne room of Almighty God and lived to tell about
it. "In the year that King Uzziah died, I saw the Lord seated on
a throne, high and exalted, and the train of his robe filled the
temple" (Isa. 6:1). Isaiah may have had this experience while he
was in the temple in Jerusalem, but in his vision he was taken
up to heaven itself.

Everything about the whole experience was designed to show
the transcendent holiness of God. God was seated in a holy
place, his kingly throne, the place of royal authority over heaven
and earth. The throne was high and lifted up to show that God
is far above his creatures. He was wearing a robe so long that it
filled the temple.

God was attended by holy angels. "Above him were seraphs,
each with six wings: With two wings they covered their faces,
with two they covered their feet, and with two they were flying"
(v. 2). These angelic beings—literally, "the burning ones"—were
holy in their own right. They had never committed the least sin.
Yet even they sensed their distance from God. Somehow they
had to acknowledge his supreme holiness. So they modestly covered their eyes and feet to shield themselves from his majesty.

Isaiah heard a holy hymn, for the seraphim "were calling to
one another: 'Holy, holy, holy is the LORD Almighty; the whole
earth is full of his glory'" (v. 3). He heard the angelic beings offer
a crescendo of praise, worshiping God for his glorious omnipotence as well as for his holiness. They repeated the word *holy*
three times in order to perfect God's praise, for the Hebrews considered three a number of completion.

Perhaps the threefold "holy" is a hint of God's triune being as Father, Son, and Holy Spirit. The well-known Reginald Heber (1783-1826) hymn based on this text connects the holiness of God with his triune being: "Holy, holy, holy! Merciful and mighty! God in three Persons, blessed Trinity!" The three-personed God is to be praised as the thrice-holy God.

The words of this holy hymn were accompanied with holy sights and sounds. "At the sound of their voices the doorposts and thresholds shook and the temple was filled with smoke" (Isa. 6:4). The angelic voices thundered. The doors of the temple shook like an earthquake, forbidding entrance. The place filled with smoke so that God's glory was shrouded in mystery.

Isaiah was as close to God as any man since Adam. Yet he was never farther away. Properly speaking, he did not even see God. These verses do not describe God at all, just the majesty surrounding him. Even when God allows a man to come into his presence, he preserves his transcendence. God is separate. He is other. He is holy, holy, holy in his holiness.

2. The second part of the story is what Isaiah felt—*himself ruined*. Many terrifying thoughts must have run through the prophet's mind when he saw God on his holy throne. He knew that no one can see God and live (Ex. 33:20). He remembered what God did to Uzziah for barging into his temple. So Isaiah was shaking in his sandals. He thought he was a dead man.

The words the prophet used to describe the way he felt are significant. "'Woe to me!' I cried. 'I am ruined!'" (Isa. 6:5a). In the previous chapter, Isaiah had pronounced six woes against the people of Jerusalem. He pronounced woe on everyone from the suburban developers (5:8) to the bar hoppers (vv. 11, 22). To the Hebrew mind, however, woes ought to come in sevens. By pronouncing only six of them, the prophet seems to leave things hanging.

Then Isaiah went to God's throne room where the divine holiness made his woes complete. "Woe is me!" he said, uttering a seventh woe. The prophet knew he was finished. He could not join the worship service or call God holy. All he could say was, "I am ruined. I am undone. I am shattered and overwhelmed. I am devastated and dismantled. It's over. I cease to exist."

3. Isaiah discovered that the holiness of God is the ruination of man. But he did not remain ruined for long, for the third part of the story is *Isaiah repentant.*

What overwhelmed the prophet was a sense of his own sin. This is what always happens when we see God as he really is: We see ourselves as we really are. We stop comparing ourselves to anyone else and become painfully aware of our distance from the Holy One. To see God in all his holiness is to see ourselves in all our sin. Isaiah said, "'Woe to me! . . . I am ruined! For I am a man of unclean lips, and I live among a people of unclean lips, and my eyes have seen the King, the LORD Almighty'" (Isa. 6:5).

It is doubtful whether Isaiah had ever repented like this before, *really* repented. Since he was a prophet, it was his job to tell other people to repent, which he did often. The reason he called people to repentance was because he had a keen sense of God's holiness. This came out in his woes against Jerusalem. Twice he called God "'the Holy One of Israel'" (Isa. 5:19, 24). Another time he said, "'the holy God will show himself holy by his righteousness'" (v. 16b).

Isaiah was already a traveling salesman for the holiness of God. But then he met the Holy One. He had talked about God's holiness. He had preached about it. He believed in it. But finally he experienced it for himself.

Notice the specific sin Isaiah confessed—unholy speech. He discovered that he was a sinner in the one area of life where he was most committed to doing God's work. Isaiah was a prophet. It was his job to go around speaking God's judgment against everyone else, and rightly so, but he did it without realizing that he himself was a foul-mouthed sinner.

It was only when he came into the light of God's holy presence that Isaiah admitted that *he* was a man of unclean lips, too.

Like King Uzziah, the leper, he had to go around saying, "Unclean! Unclean!" In other words, Isaiah was unholy. He was not separated from the sin around him; he was part of it.

This is a reminder that there is no area of life that remains unstained by sin. We are totally depraved. Even what we have consecrated to God is corrupt. As Isaiah later said, "All of us have become like one who is unclean, and all our righteous acts are like filthy rags" (64:6a). Where do you serve God best? Even there, you are unholy.

4. Isaiah knew he was unholy, too unholy to remain in the presence of the holy, holy, Holy One. But once he repented, he was *reconciled*, meaning he became a friend of God. "Then one of the seraphs flew to me with a live coal in his hand, which he had taken with tongs from the altar. With it he touched my mouth and said, 'See, this has touched your lips; your guilt is taken away and your sin atoned for'" (Isa. 6:6-7).

These two verses teach nearly everything there is to know about God's plan of salvation. The coal was taken from the altar. In other words, it came from the place of sacrifice. The altar was where a lamb was offered to God for sin. Therefore, Isaiah was reconciled to God on the basis of a blood sacrifice. This is what God always requires. Without the shedding of blood there is no remission of sin (Heb. 9:22).

Next, the sacrifice was applied directly to Isaiah's sin. Sssssssss! The coal was placed on the prophet's lips because he had sinned with his lips. Since it was a burning coal, it must have been excruciatingly painful. But it was totally effective in purging away Isaiah's sin.

The coal accomplished two things. It took away Isaiah's guilt and atoned for his sins. First, it took away the general guilt of his sin nature. Next, it atoned for his particular sins. In order for Isaiah to be reconciled to God, both things had to happen. His sin and his sins had to be dealt with. And God was the one who dealt with them. Isaiah had nothing to do with it. From beginning to end, the sinner's salvation is God's work. He accomplishes redemption, and he applies it. Thus God gives what God demands—a holy sacrifice for sin.

5. The final part of the story is *Isaiah recommissioned*. He had already begun to serve as a prophet, it seems, but this was his recommissioning: "Then I heard the voice of the Lord saying, 'Whom shall I send? And who will go for us?' And I said, 'Here am I. Send me!'" (Isa. 6:8).

This has been an inspiring verse for many Christians, especially for missionaries. "Here am I, Lord. Send me!" But Isaiah did not volunteer in a sudden act of bravado. There is no trace of self-confidence or self-righteousness in his speech. He had been through the burning. What prepared him to volunteer for God's service in verse 8 was his encounter with God's holiness in verses 1 through 7.

Isaiah was not recommissioned until he was reconciled. He could not be reconciled until he repented. He was not willing to repent until he had been ruined. Every effective servant of God must have a crushing experience of God's holiness. Concerning Isaiah, Charles Swindoll has said, "When God wants to do an impossible task, he takes an impossible man and crushes him."

Isaiah had been crushed. But once he was rescued from his ruin and reconciled to God, he became a spokesperson for God's holiness. He calls God "the Holy One" thirty times in his book, more than any other writer in the Bible. This is what he wrote, much later in life:

> For this is what the high and lofty One says—
> he who lives forever, whose name is holy:
> "I live in a high and holy place,
>   but also with him who is contrite and lowly in spirit,
> to revive the spirit of the lowly
>   and to revive the heart of the contrite. . . .
> I have seen his ways, but I will heal him;

> *I will guide him and restore comfort to him,*
> *creating praise on the lips."* (57:15, 18-19a)

That was Isaiah's experience precisely, right down to the lips. He never forgot what he saw in the throne room of heaven. He never lost his sense of God's majestic holiness. And he never stopped telling people that there was a way for unholy people to be reconciled to a holy God.

THE HOLINESS OF CHRIST

The story of Isaiah at God's holy throne is the story of everyone who comes to Jesus Christ. This is true, first of all, because Isaiah himself came to Christ.

The Gospel of John teaches that Isaiah "saw Jesus' glory and spoke about him" (John 12:41). This may simply mean that Isaiah prophesied about Jesus in a general way. But John's statement comes immediately after a quotation from Isaiah 6, the very passage in which Isaiah saw the Lord high and lifted up. What he saw on that occasion was God's glory. So when John says that Isaiah "saw Jesus' glory," he is referring to the story of Isaiah at God's holy throne. Isaiah saw the Lord Christ.

Anyone who wants to come to God must come the way Isaiah did—through Jesus Christ. Jesus is not a guru, although he is a great teacher. He is not a pop psychologist, although he knows what makes you tick. He is not a political subversive, although he did start a revolution. He is not your buddy, although he will be your friend. Jesus is not any of the things postmodern culture has tried to make him. He is the Holy One. He is very God and perfect man. In him there is no sin. To see Jesus as he is to see how holy he is.

The more you see Jesus—in all his holiness—the more you realize how unholy you are. This was not only Isaiah's experience; it was also Peter's. On one occasion Peter had been out fishing all night but had not caught so much as a single minnow.

Jesus said to him, "'Put out into deep water, and let down the nets for a catch'" (Luke 5:4). It was a ridiculous suggestion to make, especially to a fisherman. Peter reluctantly said, "All right, Jesus. If you say so." "'Master, we've worked hard all night and haven't caught anything. But because you say so, I will let down the nets'" (v. 5).

What happened, of course, was that they caught so many fish that their nets began to break, and their boats began to sink. When Peter saw this, he did something very strange. "He fell at Jesus' knees and said, 'Go away from me, Lord; I am a sinful man!'" (v. 8). This was strange because Jesus had not said anything at all about Peter's sin. But when a carpenter shows a fisherman how to fish, he must be more than a carpenter. Peter realized the vast distance that lay between him and Jesus. It was the distance between an unholy man and the holy God.

Like Isaiah, when Peter was ruined by the holiness of Jesus Christ, he repented for his sins. Then one day he was reconciled to God. He was reconciled on the basis of the blood sacrifice that Jesus offered for sins on the cross. Jesus made the holy sacrifice that took away Peter's guilt and atoned for his sins. Later, after Peter was recommissioned and began to preach about Jesus, he used Isaiah's favorite title for him—"the Holy One" (Acts 3:14).

Every unholy sinner who wants to get right with a holy God must do the same thing. You must meet Jesus Christ who is holy, holy, holy. You must see your ruin and repent for your sins. You must be reconciled to God through the death of Christ on the cross. Only then will you be of much use in God's service.

BE HOLY, BECAUSE HE IS HOLY

When the New Testament describes the followers of Jesus Christ, it often calls them "saints." In other words, Christians are "the holy ones." God "has saved us and called us to a holy life" (2 Tim. 1:9a). We are set apart for God's service. What distinguishes us from the rest of humanity is that we were chosen and created to be holy (Eph. 1:4; 4:24).

The Bible commands us to be what we are. "You ought to live holy and godly lives" (2 Peter 3:11b). "Make every effort . . . to be holy" (Heb. 12:14). "For God did not call us to be impure, but to live a holy life" (1 Thess. 4:7). The reason we are called to be holy is because the God who called us is holy. "Just as he who called you is holy, so be holy in all you do; for it is written: 'Be holy, because I am holy'" (1 Peter 1:15-16).

What does it mean to be holy?

First, a holy person talks about God's holiness, as Isaiah and Peter did. The holiness of God is part of the message of salvation. Therefore, it has an essential place in evangelism.

A Presbyterian minister took a trip to Ukraine during the 1990s. He was so impressed with the Christian work being done among university students that he asked for their philosophy of ministry. A young woman named Masha said, "You must understand, we are not afraid to hurt them in order to show them that God is more holy than they think he is and that they are more sinful." This approach to Christian witness shows profound respect for God's holiness.

A holy person hates sin. Every sin is an assault on the holiness of God. Since God himself hates sin (Ps. 5:5), so must we. The trouble with us is that, as James Montgomery Boice writes, "We do not naturally hate sin. In fact, the opposite is true. We generally love sin and are loath to part with it. But we must learn to hate sin, or else we will learn to hate God who requires a holy life from those who are Christ's followers."[4]

To be holy is not only to hate sin; it is also to love holiness in all its forms. A holy person is not just someone who does certain things and doesn't do others. A saint approaches every part of life with reverence.

A holy person loves God for his holiness. A good example is

A. W. Tozer, who wrote an entire book on the holiness of God. In one of his other books Tozer wrote:

> I tell you this: I want God to be what God is: the impeccably holy, unapproachable Holy Thing, the All-Holy One. I want Him to be and remain *THE HOLY*. I want his heaven to be holy and His throne to be holy. I don't want Him to change or modify His requirements. Even if it shuts me out, I want something holy left in the universe.[5]

Tozer's statement shows why a love for God's holiness is one of the best indicators of true Christianity. Holiness is one divine attribute that does not do us any good. As Joshua warned the children of Israel, "'You are not able to serve the LORD. He is a holy God'" (Josh. 24:19). If we love God for his holiness, it shows that we love him for who he is in himself, rather than for what he does for us.

Finally, a holy person praises God for his holiness. To do this it helps to know one more thing about Isaiah's visit to God's holy throne. His experience was a historical event. But what Isaiah saw was not simply a past event; it is a present reality.

The apostle John had the same experience Isaiah had. He went to the throne room of Almighty God. Like Isaiah he saw the Lord exalted on his heavenly throne. Around the throne he saw living creatures, each with six wings. What John heard them saying was this: "'Holy, holy, holy is the Lord God Almighty, who was, and is, and is to come'" (Rev. 4:8). Sound familiar?

The Scripture says further that those angelic creatures never stop saying, "Holy, holy, holy is the Lord God Almighty." This is their perpetual praise. They say it morning and evening. They say it day and night. They say it year after year, century after century, millennium after millennium: "Holy, holy, holy is the Lord God Almighty." They have been saying it over and over again since the year that King Uzziah died, when Isaiah saw the Lord high and lifted up.

They never stop saying it. At this very moment, those living creatures are gathered around God's heavenly throne, praising the Father, the Son, and the Holy Spirit with these words: "Holy, holy, holy is the Lord Almighty, who was, and is, and is to come." Someday—if you love God—that will be your employment as well. In the meantime, praise God in the beauty of his holiness as often as you are able.

CHAPTER 10

THE JUSTICE OF IT ALL

The Story of the First Crime and Its Punishment

—∞∞—

He is the Rock, his works are perfect,
and all his ways are just. A faithful God who does no wrong,
upright and just is he.

DEUTERONOMY 32:4

William Shakespeare's *Othello* is a tragedy of love and revenge
in which Othello, the Moor, is betrayed by Iago, his closest
counselor. Iago is a base liar. He gradually persuades Othello
that his wife, the fair Desdemona, has been unfaithful. When
Othello determines to take revenge, Iago convinces him to stran-
gle Desdemona in her bed.

Othello's response to this diabolical plan is a sad commentary on the human condition. He says, "The justice of it
pleases."[1] In fact, what Othello is about to do is a great injustice, for Desdemona loves him with all her heart. The tragedy is
that she is murdered in the name of justice.

This world is full of injustice. The innocent suffer while the
guilty go unpunished. A brutal murder remains unsolved. The
execution of a just sentence is delayed on appeal. A violent criminal gets off on a technicality. Thus the justice system often turns
out to be an injustice system.

There is injustice in the social order. The weak are crushed
by the engines of the strong. Greedy shareholders drive honest

laborers out of work. There is discrimination in the housing market. The rich get richer while the poor continue to live in poverty.

Then there are the injustices of history—invasion, slavery, persecution, terrorism, and genocide. Women and children are slaughtered while the men who gave the orders live in luxury. One people is enslaved to another. Even when they are freed, they do not receive retribution. When all these injustices are placed on the balance scales, humanity is found wanting.

THE JUDGE OF ALL THE EARTH

Justice will never be served unless there is a God. Justice demands the rendering of a judgment. Judgment, in turn, requires a judge to reward the right and punish the wrong. But in this world the right is not always rewarded, and the wrong often goes unpunished. Therefore, if there is no Final Judgment and no heaven or hell, there can be no justice. The moral books of the universe must remain forever unbalanced. No God, no justice.

Yet everyone craves justice. When people are treated unfairly, they immediately appeal to an objective standard of justice: "That's not fair!" People know injustice to be unjust because they have a sense of justice.

This innate sense of justice explains why every mystery novel ends with the crime discovered and the criminal hauled away in handcuffs. Everything must come out right in the end. It also explains why the primitive religions of the world require blood sacrifice. Almost instinctively people know that sin must be paid for, that justice must be done. But where does this sense of justice come from?

It comes from God, of course. The Bible teaches that he is the Judge, with a capital *J*. Abraham addressed him as "the Judge of all the earth" (Gen. 18:25). Moses said,

He is the Rock, his works are perfect,
and all his ways are just.
A faithful God who does no wrong,
upright and just is he. (Deut. 32:4)

The writer to the Hebrews called him "the judge of all men" (Heb. 12:23). God not only makes the laws, but he also enforces them. Thus the book of James describes him as the only "Lawgiver and Judge" (James 4:12).

God is not simply a judge; he is a just judge. "He will judge the world in righteousness; he will govern the peoples with justice" (Ps. 9:8). Speaking metaphorically, justice is a verb. To say that God is just is to say that he *does* what is right and fair. Justice is one of God's active attributes; it is something he gives.

God's justice is closely related to his wrath. Wrath is God's holy hatred of sin, what A. W. Pink calls "His eternal detestation of all unrighteousness."[2] Paul Cook gives a fuller definition:

> We would define the wrath of God as that steady displeasure and hatred which God has of sin, arising from his holiness, and expressed in his determination to punish sin according to the principles of his righteousness and justice. God's wrath is not some fickle and uncontrolled passion or outburst of anger. Human wrath is usually of this unrestrained character, frequently unjust and often violent. God's wrath is the personal expression of his holy hatred of sin and his set determination to punish it.[3]

Wrath is probably God's least popular attribute. We secretly suspect that divine wrath is not in keeping with divine love, that it is somehow unworthy of God. To quote again from A. W. Pink, "While some would not go so far as to openly admit that they consider [wrath] a blemish on the Divine character . . . they rarely hear it mentioned without a secret resentment rising up in their hearts against it."[4]

Yet God's wrath is essential to his just nature. David said, "God is a righteous judge, a God who expresses his wrath every day" (Ps. 7:11). Thus any understanding of God's justice that does not include his wrath is a misunderstanding. It is because God is just that he must be a God of wrath. This does not mean that God is irritable or cruel. Wrath is simply "God's resolute action in punishing sin."[5]

The Bible does not have the slightest inhibition about declaring that God is a God of wrath as well as mercy. This is the way he revealed himself to Moses. He began by listing his gracious attributes: "The LORD, the LORD, the compassionate and gracious God, slow to anger, abounding in love and faithfulness, maintaining love to thousands, and forgiving wickedness, rebellion and sin" (Ex. 34:6-7a).

That is where many people wish to stop. Their God is a cosmic Santa Claus, a God of unjust love. Yet the Scripture continues, "He does not leave the guilty unpunished; he punishes the children and their children for the sin of the fathers to the third and fourth generation" (v. 7b). The King James Version of this verse is even more direct when it says that God "will by no means clear the guilty."

Realize that God's just wrath is not inconsistent with his goodness. It is right and good for God to hate sin. How could he be morally indifferent? Sin is an affront to his honor. Therefore it deserves his most intense indignation. If God did not hate sin, he would not deserve our worship. The justice of God—including his wrath—is a divine perfection.

CRIME . . .

There is a story in the Bible about God's justice. It is the story of the first crime and its punishment.

There are only four characters in the story: God, the maker of heaven and earth; Adam, the man made from the dust of the ground; Eve, the mother of all the living; and Satan, the crafty serpent. The story took place in the garden God planted with his own hands, the Garden of Eden. It was the fairest of gardens, with a magnificent variety of trees heavy with fruit, and watered by flowing rivers.

Most public parks have their own rules, and the Garden of Eden was no exception. There was only one rule, almost trivial in its demand, yet asserting God's absolute authority over the garden: "'You must not eat from the tree of the knowledge of good and evil, for when you eat of it you will surely die'" (Gen. 2:17). Only one rule, and yet it came with the death penalty.

Unfortunately, Adam and Eve broke that rule. How they came to break it is a different story. In brief, the serpent tempted Eve to eat fruit from the tree of the knowledge of good and evil, and she ate. Then she shared the fruit with Adam. Immediately, they both felt something they had never felt before—shame. "Then the eyes of both of them were opened, and they realized they were naked" (3:7a).

Not only were our first parents ashamed, they were afraid. "Then the man and his wife heard the sound of the LORD God as he was walking in the garden in the cool of the day, and they hid from the LORD God among the trees of the garden" (v. 8). What they feared was God's justice. They had been warned that the wages of sin is death. Now they knew from experience what it meant to sin, and they had a fearful expectation of judgment.

Adam and Eve did everything they could to escape God's justice. They tried covering up their sin with fig leaves. They tried running away from God and hiding among the trees of the garden. They tried shifting the blame to someone else.

In short, they tried to do what human beings have tried to do with their sin ever since. We try to cover it up. We perform our most evil deeds in the dark and secret places so no one will ever find out. We try to run away from God. We fill our lives with work, sports, music, films, and all kinds of other distractions so we don't have to face him. We try to shift the blame. We claim that we are victims, or that what we did is not nearly as bad as what someone else did.

...AND PUNISHMENT

In the end all our strategies for hiding sin and avoiding guilt fail. As Adam and Eve discovered, there is no escape from God's severe and exacting justice.

God came to the garden as the righteous Judge. First he conducted his cross-examination, making a careful investigation into the facts of the case.

> The LORD God called to the man, "Where are you?"
> He answered, "I heard you in the garden, and I was afraid because I was naked; so I hid."
> And he said, "Who told you that you were naked? Have you eaten from the tree that I commanded you not to eat from?"
> The man said, "The woman you put here with me—she gave me some fruit from the tree, and I ate it."
> Then the LORD God said to the woman, "What is this you have done?" (Gen. 3:9-13a)

God's questions show that he does not judge in ignorance. He renders his judgment on the basis of the facts. But because he is all-knowing, he also knows the motives behind the facts. He is not deceived by deception. Thus he is able to give everyone what he or she deserves.

Satan got as much as he deserved. God said to him:

> "Because you have done this,
>   Cursed are you above all the livestock
>   and all the wild animals!
> You will crawl on your belly
>   and you will eat dust
>   all the days of your life.

And I will put enmity
between you and the woman,
and between your offspring and hers;
he will crush your head,
and you will strike his heel." (vv. 14-15)

This is not a speech about why snakes are legless or why people have an instinctive dread of anything that slithers. In part, it is a curse upon the serpent as an accomplice to the Fall. But it is primarily a sentence of God's judgment against Satan.

Satan is unable to soar with the angels; he must grovel in the dust of death. He is doomed to spend all of history grappling in a death struggle with humanity. He will strike at God's people, wounding the woman's seed on the heel. But eventually the devil and all his works will be destroyed.

The promise that Satan will be crushed is a gospel promise about the coming of Jesus Christ. Satan received his death blow on the cross, and it will not be long until the wound he received there crushes him altogether. We have this promise: "The God of peace will soon crush Satan under your feet" (Rom. 16:20a). This is God's justice for the diabolical deception of the devil.

God also gave justice to the woman. He said:

"I will greatly increase your pains in childbearing;
with pain you will give birth to children.
Your desire will be for your husband,
and he will rule over you." (Gen. 3:16)

Any woman who has ever given birth knows what the first part of this curse means—nine months of discomfort followed by hours of intense pain. The pain can be excruciating. My wife will never forget the birth of our firstborn, nor will I. It was such a hard delivery that I went home that night and wept.

The second part of the woman's judgment is harder to understand. What does it mean that the woman's desire will be for her husband?

This does not refer to sexual desire. Nor does it establish a hierarchy in the home. Rather, it refers to the desire for mastery and control. This is how the Hebrew word for desire is used in the very next chapter. When Cain's offering was unacceptable, God said to him, "'If you do not do what is right, sin is crouching at your door; it *desires* to have you, but you must master it'" (Gen. 4:7). In the same way that sin tried to get the upper hand on Cain, the woman will try to gain control of the man.

But that is not all. Although the woman will desire to be over the man, the man will rule the woman. This, too, is part of God's curse. The word *rule* in this case is not the word for servant leadership. It is a military word. It suggests that the man will try to attack, defeat, and even abuse the woman.

This is the justice God gave the woman for her sin. It explains the battle of the sexes in the home, the church, and society. The woman seeks to manipulate, while the man seeks to dominate. Both attitudes are accursed. Women who seek to control men and men who try to subjugate women are under God's just curse against sin.

There is further justice for the man. Whereas the woman was cursed at home, the man will be cursed in the workplace. God will make his labor laborious.

> To Adam he said, "Because you listened to your wife
>   and ate from the tree about which I commanded you,
>   'You must not eat of it,'
>   Cursed is the ground because of you;
>   through painful toil you will eat of it
>   all the days of your life.
> It will produce thorns and thistles for you,
>   and you will eat the plants of the field.
> By the sweat of your brow
>   you will eat your food

> *until you return to the ground,*
>   *since from it you were taken;*
> *for dust you are*
>   *and to dust you will return."* (Gen. 3:17-19)

That does not sound like much of a life. First you work, and then you die. The man will spend his whole life digging in the dirt. When it is all over, he will go right back into the ground he came from. This, too, is part of God's justice.

The last thing God did was drive Adam and Eve out of the garden altogether (vv. 22-24). He did it himself. God is not a modern judge who only passes sentence. Instead, he is in charge of the whole judicial process. He makes the law, investigates the crime, prosecutes the criminal, passes the sentence, and then carries out the judgment. God is legislator, investigator, prosecutor, sentencer, and executioner.

This is the story of the first crime and its punishment. Its tragic results can be read on every page of human history. The Scripture says, "The wrath of God is being revealed from heaven against all the godlessness and wickedness of men" (Rom. 1:18a). God's just sentence explains the invisible war that always rages between good and evil. It explains the pains of childbirth and the battle of the sexes. It explains the drudgery of work and the power death holds over the human race. It even explains why God seems so distant. Oh, the justice of it all!

SLOW JUSTICE

There is one mystery, however: Why didn't God execute the death sentence immediately? Although Adam became a mortal the day he sinned, he did not die right away. Yet when God told Adam not to eat from the tree he said, "'in the day that thou eatest thereof thou shalt surely die'" (Gen. 2:17 KJV). If God had given Adam summary justice, he would have been well within his rights. So why didn't he kill the man that very day?

One of the mysteries of divine justice is that it is often delayed. Occasionally, God's judgment is swift and sure. In the time it took to glance over her shoulder, Lot's wife was turned into a pillar of salt (Gen. 19:26). King Uzziah was afflicted with leprosy while he was trespassing the Holy of Holies (2 Chron. 26:19). Ananias and Sapphira were struck dead at the doors of the church (Acts 5:1-11). Herod died in his luxury box in Caesarea (Acts 12:21-23).

But it is not always this way. Sometimes God's justice is so slow in coming that one wonders if it will ever come at all. Noah preached judgment for 120 years before the flood came. The Egyptians squeezed generations of slave labor out of the Jews before the oppressors were drowned in the Red Sea. God waited centuries before he sent his rebellious people into exile in Babylon.

What is confusing about God's justice, perhaps more than anything else, is why it is so long in coming. This is part of the problem of evil. Why does it often seem to go unpunished?

The prophet Jeremiah puzzled over this. He said:

> *"You are always righteous, O LORD,*
> *when I bring a case before you.*
> *Yet I would speak with you about your justice:*
> *Why does the way of the wicked prosper?*
> *Why do all the faithless live at ease?"* (Jer. 12:1)

Jeremiah could not figure out why the wicked remain healthy and wealthy. If God is just, why doesn't he do something to punish them?

God delays his justice for many reasons. As Augustine once said, "God's ways of judgment are sometimes secret, but never unjust."[6] Sometimes he has a greater purpose to accomplish. Sometimes he is waiting for sinners to repent (2 Peter 3:9). Other times he is storing up wrath for the day of judgment (Rom. 2:5). But rest assured that God will eventually do what is just.

There is one more thing to be said about the pace of divine judgment. However slow it may seem, God's justice is never late. In the words of Jonathan Edwards (1703-1758), "A day of wrath is coming; it will come at its appointed season; it will not tarry, it shall not be delayed one moment beyond its appointed time."[7]

THE JUSTICE OF THE CROSS

In the case of the first crime and its punishment, God had a special reason to delay judgment. From the very moment Adam sinned, a death sentence hung over the human race. The blade was drawn and poised, waiting for justice to be served. All the sons of Adam and daughters of Eve were doomed to die, not just a physical death (although that was part of it), but a spiritual and eternal death.

God waited and waited, and then waited some more. Then he struck. When the blow finally fell, it fell on Jesus Christ. God carried out the death penalty against his own Son.

In one sense, the death of Christ was a great injustice, the greatest the world has ever known. Jesus was and is the perfect Son of God. He never committed the least sin, so he was convicted for a crime he did not commit. Indeed, he was convicted for a crime he *could not* commit, namely, blasphemy. He was charged with claiming to be the unique Son of God (Matt. 26:63-66). But of course he *was* the unique Son of God. Therefore, he was crucified for being exactly who he is, the Son of God and Savior of the world.

In a deeper sense, however, the death of Christ was the purest justice of all. Through that unjust crucifixion, God was actually carrying out his justice. A line from a hymn by Thomas Kelly (1769-1854)—"Stricken, Smitten, and Afflicted"—describes the situation perfectly: "but the deepest stroke that pierced him was the stroke that Justice gave."

If it were possible for God to relax his justice, surely he would have done so in order to spare his own Son. But sin cannot go unpunished. God cannot acquit the wicked. He *cannot.* In order for us to be saved, someone had to pay the just price for sin. Thomas Boston wrote, "When we hear that God exposed his own Son to the utmost severity of wrath and vengeance, may we not justly cry out 'O the infinite evil of sin! O the inflexible severity of divine justice!'"[8]

The cross of Christ is the proof of God's justice. In the cross, justice was finally served. The apostle Paul explained it like this:

> God presented him [Jesus] as a sacrifice of atonement, through faith in his blood. He did this to demonstrate his justice, because in his forbearance he had left the sins committed beforehand unpunished—he did it to demonstrate his justice at the present time, so as to be just and the one who justifies those who have faith in Jesus. (Rom. 3:25-26)

Justice was such a long time coming because God was waiting for Jesus Christ to come. Only then did he execute the death sentence our sins deserve.

THE FINAL JUDGMENT

Now, through Jesus Christ, the justice of God is a great comfort to the Christian. First, it guarantees the forgiveness of our sins. Now that Christ has died for our sins, God forgives us on the basis of his justice. Our sins have been atoned for. We have been declared righteous in the courtroom of Almighty God. In a word, we have been "justified."

Because we have been justified, God has just cause to forgive our sins. "If we confess our sins, he is faithful *and just* and will forgive us our sins and purify us from all unrighteousness"

(1 John 1:9). The cross of Christ has balanced the books. Now, on the basis of his justice as well as his mercy, God is able to forgive our sins.

Second, God's justice guarantees our reward. People sometimes say, "No good deed goes unpunished." In this fallen world, that is sometimes the case. But it will not be true in the world to come. There God will reward every kind word and every merciful deed. "God is not unjust; he will not forget your work and the love you have shown him as you have helped his people and continue to help them" (Heb. 6:10). Or again, in the words of the apostle Paul, "There is in store for me the crown of righteousness, which the Lord, the righteous Judge, will award to me on that day—and not only to me, but also to all who have longed for his appearing" (2 Tim. 4:8). Keep serving Christ, knowing that one day your service will receive its just reward.

Third, God's justice guarantees our vindication. Sometimes God's people are treated unjustly. They are persecuted precisely because they live for God. But God knows the real truth, and one day his servants will be vindicated.

When you are mistreated, hold on to the promise God gave to the Thessalonians: "God's judgment is right, and as a result you will be counted worthy of the kingdom of God, for which you are suffering. God is just: He will pay back trouble to those who trouble you and give relief to you who are troubled, and to us as well" (2 Thess. 1:5-7a). In the meantime, wait for God's justice, as Jesus did. "When they hurled their insults at him, he did not retaliate; when he suffered, he made no threats. Instead, he entrusted himself to him who judges justly" (1 Peter 2:23).

Finally, God's justice guarantees the destruction of evil. This is a wicked, wicked world. The poor are oppressed. The righteous are mistreated. The innocent are slaughtered. But one day God will right every wrong. He will punish evildoers and make the wicked pay for their cruelty. "They will have to give account to him who is ready to judge the living and the dead" (1 Peter 4:5). God will see to it that in his universe justice is done.

When will this happen?

> *This will happen when the Lord Jesus is revealed from heaven in blazing fire with his powerful angels. He will punish those who do not know God and do not obey the gospel of our Lord Jesus. They will be punished with everlasting destruction and shut out from the presence of the Lord and from the majesty of his power on the day he comes to be glorified.* (2 Thess. 1:7b-10a)

The day of God's judgment is coming. It is nearer today than it was yesterday, nearer now than it was when you began to read this sentence. It will be a great day for justice. A. W. Pink writes, "Great will be the rejoicing of the saints in that day when the Lord shall vindicate His majesty, exercise His awful dominion, magnify His justice, and overthrow the proud rebels who have dared to defy Him."[9]

This is good news for God's friends, but bad news for his enemies. Sometimes people think the idea of the final judgment is old-fashioned, that Christianity has outgrown it. As J. I. Packer notes:

> People who do not actually read the Bible confidently assure us that when we move from the Old Testament to the New, the theme of divine judgment fades into the background; but if we examine the New Testament, even in the most cursory way, we find at once that the Old Testament emphasis on God's action as Judge, far from being reduced, is actually intensified. The entire New Testament is overshadowed by the certainty of a coming day of universal judgment, and by the problem thence arising: how may we sinners get right with God while there is yet time?[10]

Packer raises the most important question of all: How can sinners get right with God while there is still time?

There will be a day of judgment, make no mistake about that. "For he [God] has set a day when he will judge the world with justice" (Acts 17:31a). And God's Word has told us what that day will be like. The final judgment will be personal and fair. "God 'will give to each person according to what he has done'" (Rom. 2:5b-6). It will be thorough and strict. "For God will bring every deed into judgment, including every hidden thing, whether it is good or evil" (Eccles. 12:14). And it will be final. Hell will serve as an eternal testimony of the justice of God's wrath against the sins of humans and demons.

Are you ready for the judgment to come? It helps to know who the judge will be. It will be Jesus Christ. The personal, fair, thorough, final adjudication of the universe "will take place on the day when God will judge men's secrets through Jesus Christ" (Rom. 2:16). The Bible plainly teaches that Jesus Christ will dispense divine justice. "He is the one whom God appointed as judge of the living and the dead" (Acts 10:42b). "For we must all appear before the judgment seat of Christ, that each one may receive what is due him for the things done while in the body, whether good or bad" (2 Cor. 5:10).

Jesus Christ is not only a loving Savior; he is also a righteous Judge. This is exactly why it is necessary to come to him now in faith, asking him to forgive your sins through his work on the cross. Otherwise you will have to pay for your sins all by yourself.

One day you will have to look into the piercing eyes of him who is the Judge of the whole universe. Will you also find him to be your Savior? I pray that you will. But you will only if you ask "the coming Judge to be your present Saviour."[11]

CHAPTER 11

GOD IS GOOD . . . ALL THE TIME

The Story of the Good Shepherd

Taste and see that the LORD is good.

PSALM 34:8A

In a book by C. S. Lewis called *The Lion, the Witch and the Wardrobe*, the Pevensie children travel to the land of Narnia, a kingdom of men and women and talking beasts. Soon they discover that Narnia is ruled by a great lion, the King of Beasts. They are not at all sure they like the idea. "Is he—quite safe?" one of them asks. "I shall feel rather nervous about meeting a lion."

The answer the children get is not the one they hoped for. Not at all. "Safe? . . . Who said anything about safe? 'Course he isn't safe. But he's good. He's the King, I tell you."[1]

The lion of Narnia shows us something true about God. The living God is not altogether safe either. He cannot be tamed. His power cannot be resisted. His justice cannot be overruled. Yet God is good. All his awesome attributes are tempered by his kindness. The same God who is holy in his wrath is gentle in his goodness.

GOD IS GOOD AND DOES GOOD

Goodness is probably God's most underrated attribute. We know how unsearchable God's wisdom is and how pristine his holiness. But goodness? It sounds like faint praise, almost like giving God a B instead of an A+. God is not just good; he's great!

If the goodness of God is underrated, it is because the word *good* has been put in the bargain bin of the English language. Nobody advertises anything "good" anymore; it always has to be something "better" or "new and improved." Unless something is "totally awesome," it will never sell.

God *is* awesome, of course, but he is also good, just plain old good. There is nothing bad about him. He is good all the way through. He will always be good. "Give thanks to the LORD, for he is good; his love endures forever" (Ps. 107:1).

There are two ways of talking about divine goodness, and they appear together in a verse from the Psalms: "You are good, and what you do is good" (Ps. 119:68a). God is good and does good. He is good in relationship to himself, and he is good in relationship to us.

First, God is good in and of himself. It is God's very nature and essence to be good. Even if he had never done anything, he would still be the God Augustine called "the Supreme Good." This is how the Puritan Thomas Manton (1620-1677) explained God's essential goodness:

> He is originally good, good of Himself, which nothing else is; for all creatures are good only by participation and communication from God. He is essentially good; not only good, but goodness itself: the creature's good is a superadded quality, in God it is His essence. He is infinitely good; the creature's good is but a drop, but in God there is an infinite ocean or gathering together of good. He is eternally and immutably good, for He cannot be less good than He is; as there can be no addition made to Him, so no subtraction from Him.[2]

God is infinitely, absolutely, and unchangeably good in himself.

God is also infinitely good to us, which is a second way to

talk about his goodness. He not only *is* good, but he also *does* good. The two are closely related, of course. The reason God does good is because he is good. The Dutch theologian Herman Bavinck thus defines goodness as "that perfection in God which prompts Him to deal bountifully and kindly with all His creatures."[3]

Everything God has ever done is good. His creation is good (very good, in fact). His creatures are good. His law is good. His plans are good. His ways are good. Moreover, God does all these good things for our benefit. The prophet Isaiah said:

> I will tell of the kindnesses of the LORD,
>   the deeds for which he is to be praised,
>   according to all the LORD has done for us—
> yes, the many good things he has done
>   for the house of Israel,
>   according to his compassion and
> many kindnesses (Isa. 63:7).

As we saw near the beginning of this book, there was a time when God showed Moses all his goodness. The prophet heard God's voice say, "'The LORD, the LORD, the compassionate and gracious God, slow to anger, abounding in love and faithfulness'" (Ex. 34:6). Compassion, grace, love, and faithfulness—together these qualities make up God's goodness. To quote again from Herman Bavinck, goodness is not so much an attribute by itself as it is "the sum-total of all perfections."[4]

God has taken his perfect goodness and scattered it throughout the universe. He is good not only to his friends, but also to his enemies. "The LORD is good to all; he has compassion on all he has made" (Ps. 145:9). J. I. Packer explains the psalmist's point: "Since God controls all that happens in His world, every meal, every pleasure, every possession, every bit of sun, every night's sleep, every moment of health and safety, everything else that sustains and enriches life, is a divine gift."[5]

Everything good comes from God. This is what Jesus meant when he said that God alone is good (Mark 10:18). There are other things that are good, of course, but they get all their goodness from God. He alone is the origin and source of all goodness. Every other good comes secondhand.

A GOOD FRIEND

The goodness of God is a vast and inexhaustible subject. In his classic work on the divine attributes, Stephen Charnock devoted no less than 100 dense pages to the subject.[6] But there is a story in the Bible to teach us about God's goodness. It is the story of the Good Shepherd.

Different parts of the Good Shepherd's story appear in different places in the Bible, but the place to begin is the twenty-third psalm. Psalm 23 was written by David, who was a shepherd in his own right. The psalm begins with deity and ends with eternity; in between, it is all about the goodness of God. David lists one good thing after another to show that God is everything a sheep could ever want in a shepherd.

First, the Good Shepherd is a *good friend*. The psalm begins with the special name God revealed to Moses: "Lord," or "Yahweh," or "Jehovah." He is the Great I AM, the self-existent and self-sufficient one, who does not depend on anyone else for help.

The wonderful thing is that this great God is who he is in relationship to me. "The LORD is *my* shepherd" (v. 1). The all-wise and all-powerful holy Judge of the universe has entered into a friendship with me. The Great I AM is my Good Shepherd.

I first learned Psalm 23 from my father. I can still remember lying in bed, with the covers tucked around me, repeating his words: "'The Lord is my shepherd, I shall not want.'" I remember, too, the warm, joyous, peaceful feeling of being with Jesus when I said the psalm.

I say "with Jesus" because it is impossible to understand Psalm 23 without recognizing that Jesus is the Good Shepherd. Jesus said to his disciples, "'I am the good shepherd'" (John 10:11a). It was a way of saying to them, "Look, everything you ever read about shepherds in the Bible—Psalm 23 and all the rest of it—is really about me. *I am* the Good Shepherd."

One thing that makes Jesus a good shepherd is that he knows his sheep. And his sheep know him. The difference between a shepherd and a stranger is that the sheep know the shepherd's voice. "'He calls his own sheep by name and leads them out . . . and his sheep follow him because they know his voice'" (John 10:3-4). All the sheep in God's flock know the voice of Jesus Christ, the Good Shepherd.

Everyone is looking for good relationships these days. Old people are looking for friends to care for them. Young people are looking for friends to accept them. Married people are looking for friends who won't make too many demands on them. Single people are looking for friends who will stay committed to them. Everyone is looking for a few good friends.

Out of his goodness, Jesus offers what everyone is looking for—a warm, stable, committed, accepting relationship. If you can truly say, "The Lord is my shepherd," then you have a good friendship with a good God.

GOOD FOOD AND GOOD DRINK

Among the many gifts God gives to his friends are *good food and good drink*.

> *The LORD is my shepherd,*
> *I shall not be in want.*
> *He makes me lie down in green pastures,*
> *he leads me beside quiet waters.* (Ps. 23:1-2)

The Good Shepherd is a good provider. His sheep lack nothing because he lacks nothing. This is important because sheep cannot care for themselves. Not that their needs are complex. Sheep do not have gourmet appetites. But there are two things they must have—green grass and fresh water, specifically still water, since sheep will not drink from a running stream.

When I think of green pastures, I think of a meadow I saw in the Big Horn Mountains of Montana. We drove up a winding road through jagged rocks. When we reached the plateau, we found ourselves in a field of green grass and bright flowers, dancing red and yellow in the sun.

When I think of quiet waters, I think of the channel off Long Lake in the Wisconsin North Woods. Hour after hour, the stream slips quietly by, unhurried, and the frogs on the lily pads rest undisturbed.

You probably have favorite streams and meadows of your own. Wherever they are, they are the kind of green pastures and quiet waters where the Good Shepherd leads his sheep. These sheep do not just eat; they eat the choicest morsels of grass. They do not just drink; they drink from fresh springs in the rock-dry desert.

This is the kind of refreshment people find in Jesus Christ. Jesus said, "'He who comes to me will never go hungry, and he who believes in me will never be thirsty'" (John 6:35). He was speaking spiritually, of course. Jesus satisfies the desperate hunger and thirst of the human soul.

If you are one of God's sheep, do not doubt the goodness of God's care. In his goodness, Jesus knows what you need; out of his goodness he will provide it. Charles Spurgeon (1834-1892) wrote, "We must never tolerate an instant's unbelief as to the goodness of the Lord; whatever else may be questioned, this is absolutely certain, that Jehovah is good; His dispensations may vary, but His nature is always the same."[7]

A GOOD REST

Once they have been fed well, sheep like to lie down for a *good rest*, as the sheep of the Good Shepherd are able to do. They lie down in green pastures.

One of the most helpful books on Psalm 23 was written by a former shepherd named Phillip Keller. Keller explains that sheep will not lie down unless four conditions are met. They must be free from fear of predators. They must be free from friction with other sheep. They must be free from flies and other pests. And they must be free from famine. Only then are they able to rest.[8]

What this means is that sheep cannot rest unless they have a good shepherd. They depend on their shepherd to feed them and keep them safe. They will have no rest unless he does this.

The same is true in the spiritual life. The only place we can find true rest is in God's pasture. Only God can satisfy. Our rest depends on his goodness. I sometimes reflect on this as I read the Bible verse on my bedroom wall: "Be at rest once more, O my soul, for the LORD has been good to you" (Ps. 116:7).

David's soul was at rest in God's goodness. He was able to say, "he restores my soul" (Ps. 23:3a). Souls often need to be restored. We feel empty and disappointed. We are weighed down by sorrow and grief. We grow weary and discouraged. But God is the one who restores the soul. He does not do this by offering a five-step plan for spiritual renewal. He *is* the renewer. As we turn away from sin and toward him, he restores us from the inside out. If we find that we are not at rest, it is because we are not resting in God's goodness.

Good rest comes to us through Jesus Christ, who said, "'Come to me, all you who are weary and burdened, and I will give you rest. Take my yoke upon you and learn from me, for I am gentle and humble in heart, and you will find rest for your souls'" (Matt. 11:28-29).

When David mentioned the way God restored his soul, he was talking about something more than renewal. He was also talking about being rescued. The Hebrew word for restore is actually a word for rescue. It is used that way at the beginning of Psalm 60: "You have rejected us, O God, and burst forth upon us; you have been angry—now restore us!" (v. 1).

Sheep often need to be rescued. Sometimes they wander into danger. Sometimes they get stuck. They fall over onto their sides or backs and cannot regain their feet. Phillip Keller describes the pathetic sight: "Lying on its back, its feet in the air, it flays [sic] away frantically struggling to stand up, without success. Sometimes it will bleat a little for help, but generally it lies there lashing about in frightened frustration. If the owner does not arrive on the scene within a reasonably short time, the sheep will die."[9] Only the shepherd can restore the sheep to an upright position.

In its spiritual sense, to be restored is to be rescued from a life of sin. This, too, is the work of the Good Shepherd.

A sad article appeared in the *Philadelphia Inquirer* in November of 1998. It described the plight of the forgotten street children of Romania. One child said:

> My mother is in Bucharest somewhere. But I can't find her. My stepfather who used to beat me is dead. I can't go home because I don't know where it is. I don't know why my mother left me. I'm mad at her. But I think God helps me. God has a great heart. He thinks about me. I hope he will give me a better chance. I know the devil forced me here and God just has to find me.[10]

I do not know whether God ever found that child or not. I pray that he did. What I do know is that it is the Good Shepherd's joy to find his lost sheep. When we are lost in our sins, he is the one who finds us and brings us back.

This is a reminder that Jesus is the kind of shepherd who goes out to look for lost sheep and bring them back home. This is the meaning of the "Parable of the Found Sheep" (Luke 15:3-7). The Good Shepherd leaves ninety-nine sheep out in the open country to go and find one lost sheep. Psalm 23 records the testimony of that sheep, once he has been found: "He restoreth my soul."

GOOD DIRECTIONS

A good friend. Good food and drink. A good rest. What else is good about the Good Shepherd? He gives *good directions.* "He guides me in paths of righteousness for his name's sake" (Ps. 23:3b).

There is a big difference between good directions and bad ones. Usually it is the difference between getting lost and getting where you want to go. The Good Shepherd gets his sheep where they need to go.

His guidance is necessary, of course, because sheep tend to wander more than any other livestock. Given the opportunity, they will meander aimlessly over the hills and far away. Human beings are the same way. "We all, like sheep, have gone astray, each of us has turned to his own way" (Isa. 53:6a).

This explains why so many people are looking for guidance and direction. Non-Christian people are looking for meaning and significance in life. Christian people think they know what life means, but they don't always know what to do with it. Where should I go to school? Which job should I accept? Should I get married? Whom should I marry? What should I do with the rest of my life?

Those are not easy questions, but the Good Shepherd promises good guidance. F. W. Boreham writes, "Without his skilful leadership, the cleverest sheep would become hopelessly lost; following his footsteps, the silliest sheep cannot miss the way."[11] The guidance he gives does not tell us what to do in any and every situation. His direction is much more helpful than that. It teaches the difference between right and wrong. By his word, the Good Shepherd teaches his sheep the difference between the right path and the wrong path.

A GOOD COMPANION

Sometimes even the right path proves to be dangerous, which is why sheep need their shepherd to stay with them, as their *good companion*.

> *Even though I walk*
> *through the valley of the shadow of death,*
> *I will fear no evil,*
> *for you are with me;*
> *your rod and your staff,*
> *they comfort me.* (Ps. 23:4)

This promise of safety assumes the presence of danger. All God's sheep must pass through death's dark shadow. We are mortal, and so are the people we love. Death is our common enemy. Even when we follow God's leading, we face the loss of life.

F. B. Meyer imagines the situation like this:

The Shepherd is conducting His flock toward their fold in luxuriant pastures and in quiet resting-places. But suddenly the path turns downward, and begins to wind toward the ravine below. On the one side is a precipice, yawning in sheer descent to the steep river bed, where the water foams and roars, torn by jagged rocks. On the other side the mountain firs cast a sombre shadow in the deepening twilight. The path still plunges downward until it passes into a deep and narrow gorge overhung by the frowning battlements of rock. . . .[12]

Yet through it all, the Good Shepherd stays with his sheep. The closeness of his presence is emphasized by the change of address in verse 4. Up until now, David has described God in the third person: *He* makes me lie down; *he* restores my soul; *he* guides me; and so forth. But when David passes through the valley of the shadow of death, he speaks directly to the shepherd: "*You* are with me."

It is as if the shepherd has turned back to help his sheep. Up on the green meadow it was comfort enough simply to follow the Good Shepherd. But down in death's dark vale a sheep needs his shepherd by his side. The shepherd is right there, offering protection not only from danger, but also from the fear of danger, which is often worse than the danger itself.

Sooner or later death will cast its shadow on your path. But when you walk through death's dark valley, you will not walk alone. The Good Shepherd will walk with you. He will help you the most when you need the most help. And with him by your side, you will take the valley in your stride. You will fear no evil. You will walk through the valley to the other side.

The words of Psalm 23 have been a great comfort to many Christians at death. Two of the most famous were Isobel Alison and Marion Harvey, young Scottish women who were martyred for their faith in 1681. As they emerged from their cell, they were told to walk to the gallows at the far end of the prison yard.

"Come on, Bell," said Marion, "we can't walk in silence! This is our great day! Let us sing!" She started up the metrical version of the Twenty-third Psalm. As the two women mounted the steps of the scaffold, they sang:

> "*Yea, though I walk in death's dark vale,*
> *Yet will I fear no ill:*
> *For Thou art with me; and Thy rod*
> *And staff me comfort still.*"[13]

The mention of the rod and the staff serves as a reminder that God's goodness includes *good discipline*. The shepherd's rod and staff have many uses. The rod is worn at the shepherd's belt. It can be used as a club to defend sheep from lions and wolves. The staff is held in the shepherd's hand. It keeps sheep on the right path and lifts them to safety. Thus the rod and the staff are used for many of the good things David has already mentioned—protection, guidance, and rescue.

But the rod and the staff (especially the rod) are also used to correct and discipline the sheep. They are symbols of the shepherd's authority. Sometimes he has to strike wayward sheep to keep them from straying. This does not harm the sheep. Actually, it helps keep them safe.

In the same way, correction and rebuke are proofs of God's goodness. His rod and staff are a comfort to us because they show that he loves us too much to let us wander off on our own. The Good Shepherd says, "'Those whom I love I rebuke and discipline'" (Rev. 3:19).

A GOOD END

It is sometimes suggested that Psalm 23 ends with a change of scenery. Sheep are left behind for the world of human relationships, as the word *enemies* seems to suggest:

> *You prepare a table before me*
> *in the presence of my enemies.*
> *You anoint my head with oil;*
> *my cup overflows.* (Ps. 23:5)

Yet the case can be made that David is still writing from the sheep's point of view. Indeed, most shepherds think this verse applies to sheep. Before a shepherd takes his flock into a new field, they say, he must first prepare it by digging up any poisonous plants. This is especially true when the sheep move to the high plateaus, or tablelands, for the summer.

The anointing oil and the overflowing cup are also part of a sheep's experience. This is how one shepherd describes the ancient custom:

> At every sheepfold there is a big earthen bowl of olive oil and a large jar of water. As the sheep come in for the night, they are led to a gate. . . . as each sheep passes, he [the shepherd] quickly examines it for briars in the ears, snags in the cheek or weeping of the eyes from dust or scratches. . . . Each sheep's wounds are carefully cleaned. Then the shepherd dips his hand into the olive oil and anoints the injury. A large cup is dipped into the jar of water, kept cool by evaporation in the unglazed pottery, and is brought out—never half full but always overflowing. The sheep will sink its nose into the water clear to the eyes, if fevered, and drink until fully refreshed.[14]

If that is the way these verses are to be understood, then Psalm 23 ends back at the sheepfold.

The Dutch artist Anton Mauve produced a wonderful painting called *The Return of the Flock* (ca. 1886-1887). The painting depicts a flock of sheep heading home through the fields along a wide track. There are dozens of sheep of all sizes and descriptions. They are viewed from the rear, and the perspective of the painting makes the shepherd its focal point. All the sheep are following their shepherd home.

Home is where the sheep of the Good Shepherd end up. They come to a *good end*. Into green pastures, beside still waters, down right paths, and through dark valleys, the shepherd leads his sheep home. There is nothing else they need or desire. They want nothing. As they reflect on their experiences they reach this conclusion: "Surely goodness and love will follow me all the days of my life, and I will dwell in the house of the LORD forever" (v. 6).

The word for "love" is especially significant. It is really the word for "lovingkindness" or "covenant mercy." F. B. Meyer notes that God's goodness and mercy always go together. "Not goodness alone; for we are sinners needing forgiveness. Not mercy alone; for we need many things besides forgiveness. But each with the other linked. Goodness to supply every want; mercy to forgive every sin: goodness to provide; mercy to pardon."[15]

When God shows his goodness to sinners, the proper word for it is *grace*. Grace is God's goodness to undeserving sinners. We should never forget that the goodness of his grace comes to us through the death of Jesus Christ on the cross. Jesus said, "'I am the good shepherd. The good shepherd lays down his life for the sheep'" (John 10:11). Of all the good things the Good Shepherd does, his sacrifice is the best thing of all.

Since God has been so good to us, we must be good to others. We should be good to them in the same ways the Good Shepherd has shown us his goodness. We should be good friends. We should share good food and good drink. We should give people good rest. We should give them good directions from God's Word. We should walk with them through the valley of the shadow of death. We should do all these things because God has shown us his goodness in Jesus Christ.

Divine goodness will follow us all the days of our lives. It is sometimes suggested that there is no heaven in the Old Testament, that the Hebrews had no doctrine of the afterlife. Psalm 23 teaches just the opposite. The psalm ends with David's conviction that he will live in God's house "into the ages," meaning forever. God is good all the time and for all times.

The assurance of God's goodness explains why the Twenty-third Psalm was so often sung by Scottish immigrants when they left for America.[16] Imagine the scene: A ship loaded with goods and passengers, bound for the New World. On the shore, hundreds of well-wishers, waving their hats and shouting good-bye to family members they would never see again on this earth.

As the ship pulled away from the dock, all the people would sing the Twenty-third Psalm. The closing stanza, especially, must have caused a lump to swell in many a throat: "Surely goodness and mercy shall follow me all the days of my life: and I will dwell in the house of the LORD for ever" (Ps. 23:6 KJV).

CHAPTER 12

NOTHING BUT THE TRUTH

The Story of Jesus Before Pilate

———⚬∞⚬———

I, the LORD, speak the truth; I declare what is right.

ISAIAH 45:19C

Not long ago a certain head of state complained that his people were living in a "contaminated moral environment." Of all the vices he observed in his culture, the one that troubled him most was lying. His country seemed trapped in what he called a "web of mendacity," a tangled web of lies.

The man who said these things was not an American. He was Václav Havel, the former president of the Czech Republic, and he described his society like this:

> Because the regime is captive to its own lies, it must falsify everything. It falsifies the past, it falsifies the present, and it falsifies the future. It falsifies statistics. It pretends not to possess an omnipotent and unprincipled police apparatus. It pretends to respect human rights. It pretends to persecute no one. It pretends to fear nothing. It pretends to pretend nothing.[1]

Havel was describing life in communist Czechoslovakia. But his words show what happens to any culture that exchanges the truth for a lie.

PEOPLE OF THE LIE

We are not living in truthful times. This book has been organized around the definition of God from the Westminster Shorter Catechism: "God is a Spirit, infinite, eternal, and unchangeable in his being, wisdom, power, holiness, justice, goodness, and truth." That definition ends with the divine attribute that is perhaps most under attack in these postmodern times—truth.

Not long ago the world was a place where some things were true and other things were false. People didn't always agree what the truth was, but at least they knew what they were arguing about. One and only one of them had the truth.

Now people wonder whether anything is true at all. The truth is not what happened; it is what sells. What is true for you may not be true for me. Truth is no longer stranger than fiction; it *is* a fiction. This is an age, writes Alistair Begg, in which "plausibility is given to every idea, and certainty to none."[2]

There is little truth in advertising. The commercials and the billboards entice us with false and unattainable ideals of wealth and beauty. Almost every ad is an exaggeration.

There is little truth in politics. Public trust in national leaders is at an all-time low. The nation's capital has become one long criminal investigation. In an essay called "Lies My Presidents Told Me," Richard Stengel observes that "in Washington lying is an art form and a growth industry. . . . We're defining deception downward."[3]

The postmodern attitude about truth in politics was demonstrated perhaps most clearly during President William Jefferson Clinton's testimony before a grand jury. In one of his attempts to evade the truth he said, "It depends on what your definition of the word *is* is." When people are not sure what *is* is, they do not know what truth is.

Globally, truth is in short supply. As former Secretary of

Defense Donald Rumsfeld wrote, "It's a big world, a complicated one, and deception and denial are pervasive."[4]

There is little truth in law. The legal system used to be based
on factual evidence adjudicated according to timeless moral
truths. This is becoming less and less true, as Suzanna Sherry and
Daniel A. Farber have shown in a book called *Beyond All
Reason: The Radical Assault on Truth in American Law*.[5]

There is little truth in telecommunications or the media. The
Internet is a vast web of rumor, conspiracy, and false identity. In
journalism, fact is often blended with opinion. One wonders
what would happen if all the mistakes, mistruths, and misleading statements were taken out of the daily newspaper. How
many pages would be left?

There is little truth in theology, where postmodern theologians deny the possibility of stating true propositions about God
and salvation. They are trying to present what they call a "Christ
without Absolutes."[6] Such a Christ is no Christ at all. Yet he is
preached from many pulpits.

Then there are all the lies we tell one another. Consider how
many terms there are for different kinds of untruth. There are
lies, fibs, deceptions, falsehoods, fabrications, falsifications, pre-
varications, and misrepresentations. Most crimes—from forgery
to perjury—involve an element of deceit.

Lying is one sin nearly everyone agrees is still a sin. It is also
one sin everyone commits, probably because it is so easy. We tell
lies at home, at work, and even at church. "We fool others in
order to fool ourselves, and we fool ourselves in order to fool
others."[7] One study concluded that typical Americans lie to
nearly one-third of the people they talk to in a given week.[8]

So whom can you trust to tell the plain, honest truth? Your
friends? Your lawyer? Your newscaster? Your employer? Your
insurance carrier? Your president? Your pastor? Anyone? As it
was in the days of the prophets, "Truth is nowhere to be found"

(Isa. 59:15a). "Friend deceives friend, and no one speaks the truth" (Jer. 9:5a).

WHAT IS TRUTH?

In a world of lies, people are still looking for the truth. The difficulty of that quest was illustrated by the television program "The X-Files," which first aired in the mid-1990s. From time to time, one of the main characters would say, "The truth is out there." The truth may be out there, but where is it? And what is it?

What is the truth? The Roman governor Pontius Pilate found himself asking the same question early one morning. A group of Jewish leaders were standing outside his palace in Jerusalem, asking for an audience. They had brought with them a prisoner, a man from Nazareth named Jesus.

The governor was no friend of the Jews (particularly at that hour of the morning!), so he asked them what their business was. "Pilate came out to them and asked, 'What charges are you bringing against this man?'" (John 18:29).

In fact, the Jewish leaders had the same question themselves. They had been up all night trying to figure out what crime Jesus had committed. All they knew was that he was such a nuisance they wanted to get rid of him. Since they were not sure quite what to tell Pilate, they ended up lying about it. "'If he were not a criminal,' they replied, 'we would not have handed him over to you'" (v. 30).

It was a clever lie, the kind of lie it takes a lawyer, a politician, or maybe a theologian to come up with. It was a way of alleging that Jesus was a criminal without actually stating what his crime was. But Pontius Pilate was not deceived. One of the other Gospels explains that "he knew it was out of envy that they had handed Jesus over to him" (Matt. 27:18). So he told the priests to judge Jesus according to their own laws.

That suggestion did not satisfy the priests. "'But we have no right to execute anyone,' the Jews objected" (John 18:31b). This was true, and it also revealed their true motives. They wanted Jesus dead. The problem was that they did not have the right to carry out the death penalty.

By this point Pilate realized that it was not going to be easy to get rid of the angry mob outside his palace. In order to get to the bottom of it all, he summoned Jesus into the palace and started to conduct his own investigation: "'Are you the king of the Jews?'" (v. 33); "'What is it you have done?'" (v. 35). Pilate wanted to know the truth.

Jesus gave the governor some honest answers. He *was* a king, but not the kind of king Pilate was used to. "'My kingdom is not of this world. If it were, my servants would fight to prevent my arrest by the Jews. But now my kingdom is from another place'" (v. 36).

As he so often did, Jesus was talking in riddles. Pilate really had no idea what Jesus was saying, but at least he had his answer. "'You are a king, then!' said Pilate" (v. 37a).

It was true. Jesus was a king. "'You are right in saying I am a king,'" he admitted. "'In fact, for this reason I was born, and for this I came into the world, to testify to the truth. Everyone on the side of truth listens to me'" (v. 37b).

At this mention of truth, Pilate raised his famous question: "'What is truth?'" (v. 38). It was a skeptical question, the kind of question people raise during a trial when they despair of ever finding out the truth.

There are two sad things about Pilate's question. One is that he refused to wait for an answer. Sir Francis Bacon (1561–1626) began his essay "Of Truth" with these famous words: "*What is truth?* said jesting Pilate, and would not stay for an answer."[9] Bacon had obviously read his Gospels. "'What is truth?' Pilate asked. With this he went out again to the Jews" (v. 38). Although he asked the question, he did not expect to get an answer. It was his way of putting off making a commitment. If you really want to know what the truth is, sometimes you have to wait around for the answer.

LET GOD BE TRUE

The other sad thing about Pilate's question is that the truth was staring him in the face. Literally. If he wanted to know the truth, well, there it was. When Pilate asked for truth, the truth was standing right in front of him in the person of Jesus Christ.

Jesus knew what the truth was. He had come to testify to it, to explain to people what it was. That is why he came into this world and why he was born in Bethlehem. People sometimes ask about the "true meaning of Christmas." The only time Jesus addressed that issue, he explained it like this: "'For this reason I was born, and for this I came into the world, to testify to the truth'" (John 18:37).

Jesus was born to tell us the truth. This is why so many of his statements recorded in the Gospels begin with the words, "Verily, verily," or "I tell you the truth." Jesus always told the truth, and he would have told Pilate the truth, too, if only the man had waited to hear it.

What would Jesus have told him?

I suppose Jesus would have begun by telling Pilate that the truth is God himself. Not long before, Jesus had called his Father "'the only true God'" (John 17:3). He is "the true God" (2 Chron. 15:3), and the true God is the "God of truth" (Ps. 31:5). Veracity is one of his essential attributes. There is nothing false about him.

The truth of God refers to the integrity of his character. God is who he says he is. God cannot deny himself (2 Tim. 2:13). As J. I. Packer explains:

Truth in the Bible is a quality of persons primarily, and of propositions only secondarily: it means stability, reliability, firmness, trustworthiness, the quality of a person who is entirely self-consistent, sincere, realistic, and undeceived. God is such a person: truth, in this sense, is His nature, and He has not got it in Him to be anything else.[10]

One way to tell that God is true is by the way he appeals to his own truthfulness. For example, when God gave his promises to Abraham, he said, "'I swear by myself'" (Gen. 22:16). Human beings always swear by some greater truth. In a court of law witnesses swear on the Bible. We cannot swear by ourselves because we are prone to be false.

But God swears by himself. There is no greater truth for him to swear by (Heb. 6:13). He *is* the Truth! As the Scripture says, "Let God be true, and every man a liar" (Rom. 3:4). This is what Jesus might have said to Pilate about the true God.

Jesus also might have explained that because God is the Truth, all truth comes from him. He is the origin, the source, and the ground of all truth. All truth is God's truth, wherever it may be found. As the theologian Herman Bavinck put it, God is "the Truth, in whom and from whom and through whom all things are true which are true."[11]

Since God is true, his words are true. Jesus came to testify about this as well. In the previous chapter he said, "Thy word is truth" (John 17:17 KJV). This only makes sense. If God himself is true, then his words must be "trustworthy and true" (Rev. 22:6). "The word of the LORD is right and true; he is faithful in all he does" (Ps. 33:4).

The Bible is "the word of truth" (Ps. 119:43). Daniel called it "the Book of Truth" (Dan. 10:21). It is the true Word of God truly written, written by the "Spirit of truth" (John 14:17). It is inerrant: It does not err. It is infallible: It cannot err. It is eternal: It will not err. "All your words are true," wrote the psalmist; "all your righteous laws are eternal" (Ps. 119:160).

The Bible is reliable from beginning to end. Its history is true history. Its prophecies are true, and many have been confirmed already. Its poetry is true to human experience. Its laws are true to God's will (Ps. 119:151). Its promises are true, for "he who promised is faithful" (Heb. 10:23). What science it contains is also true, true to human observation.

All the doctrines in the Bible are true, from the creation to the consummation. These doctrines teach "a faith and knowledge resting on the hope of eternal life, which God, who does not lie, promised before the beginning of time" (Titus 1:2). The truth of Christianity thus depends on the fact that God is not a liar.

In his Word God tells the truth about salvation. He says that all your sins can be forgiven through the death and resurrection of Jesus Christ. This is "the truth of the gospel" (Gal. 2:5; cf. Eph. 1:13). Anyone who believes this truth receives true life from the true God.

JESUS *IS* THE TRUTH

All of this is what Jesus might have said to Pilate—that God's Word, like God himself, is true. But remember that all of God's attributes are displayed in Jesus Christ. Therefore, if Pilate had bothered to wait for an answer, Jesus undoubtedly would have gone on to explain that he himself *is* the truth.

In a way, Pilate was asking the wrong question. He wanted to know *what* the truth is, but the real question is *who* the truth is. The answer is that Jesus Christ is the truth. The Dutch art critic H. R. Rookmaaker explains the significance of this:

> Christ *is* the truth—a fact which is seldom sufficiently considered or appreciated. Truth is more than conceptual truth, for truth in the last analysis is personal. Christ as the truth is the Lamb of God, the agent of God's grace and of the renewal of creation, yet also the one who is to rule all the nations with a rod of iron.[12]

Or, as William Walsham How (1823-1897) put it in one of his hymns, Jesus is the "Truth unchanged, unchanging."

This is a claim the Bible often makes about Jesus, especially in the writings of John. "The Word became flesh," John wrote, referring to Jesus, "and made his dwelling among us. We have seen his glory, the glory of the One and Only, who came from the Father, full of grace and truth" (John 1:14). "Grace and truth came through Jesus Christ" (v. 17a). "We are in him who is true—even in his Son Jesus Christ. He is the true God and eternal life" (1 John 5:20).

The reason John made this truth claim about Jesus is that Jesus made it about himself. When his disciples asked him the way to heaven, he said, "'I am the way and the truth and the life'" (John 14:6). The striking thing about this claim is its use of the definite article. Jesus claims to be *the* truth. He is the only way, the only truth, the only life. The Truth, therefore, is what God knows to be true in Jesus Christ.

It is this aspect of Christianity—the exclusivity of Jesus Christ—that is more offensive to the secular mind than any other. The postmodern age has lost its confidence in truth. There are no facts, only feelings; no truths, only interpretations.

If you want, you may even make up your own truth. There is only one thing you are not allowed to do, and that is claim that you have the only truth. A generation ago people objected to Christianity by saying it wasn't true. Now people object to it for having the audacity even to claim to be true. If Christianity is true at all, people say, it is only relatively true.

There is a striking example of postmodern attitudes about religious truth on the campus of Vanderbilt University. In 1993 Vanderbilt built a shrine to religious relativism called the All Faith Chapel. It is designed to be used by Jews, Christians, Hindus, Muslims, and whatever other religious groups happen to be on campus.

A prisoner once wrote to tell me that the same thing has hap-

pened in America's federal prisons. His prison chapel is deco-
rated with a cross, a menorah, a star and crescent, and other religious symbols.

Consider what these chapels say about truth. They say that
truth is relative, that no religion is any more true than any other.
But that is really a way of saying that every religion is false.
Christians believe that there is only one God who exists in three
persons. Hindus worship several hundred thousand deities.
Buddhists do not believe in a personal God at all. Which religion
is right? The religions of the world hold contradictory views on
the nature and being of God. If one claims that they are all right,
then by the same reasoning they are all wrong, and faith in God
becomes just another personal preference.

Jesus Christ refuses to share worship space with any other
deity. He is not merely one part of the truth. When it comes to
having a relationship with God, Jesus is the truth, the whole
truth, and nothing but the truth.

God has given one and only one Savior to the world. "God
so loved the world that he gave his one and only Son, that whoever believes in him shall not perish but have eternal life" (John
3:16). The only way to gain eternal life is to believe in Jesus
Christ. "Whoever believes in him is not condemned, but whoever does not believe stands condemned already because he has
not believed in the name of God's one and only Son" (v. 18).

Christians have always taught and believed that Jesus Christ
is the unique Savior of the world. This is part of what the
Reformers meant when they spoke of salvation by grace alone,
through faith alone, in Christ alone. During the Zurich
Disputations of 1523, the Swiss Reformer Ulrich Zwingli
(1484-1531) said, "The summary of the gospel is that our Lord
Jesus Christ, the true Son of God, has revealed the will of his
heavenly Father to us, and with his innocence has redeemed us
from death, and has reconciled us with God. Therefore, Christ

is the only way to salvation for all those who have been, are, and will be."[13]

Jesus is the only true way to God. Every other way is false.

TO TELL THE TRUTH

If Jesus is the truth, then he forces everyone to make a choice. There is no middle ground with him. He demands to be worshiped as the unique Son of God and the Savior of the world. That is not the kind of claim you can just ignore. You can either accept it or reject it, but you must decide one way or the other.

People were never ambivalent about Jesus of Nazareth. Either they loved him or they hated him. Either they wanted to crown him or to crucify him. That was exactly the choice Pilate was forced to make. Jesus said to him, "'Everyone on the side of truth listens to me'" (John 18:37b). This was a way of asking Pilate whose side he was on. "Which will it be, Pontius? Are you for me or against me?"

Jesus forces us to make the same choice. Are you for him or against him? Will you follow him, or will you turn your back on him?

We live in a culture that does not like to choose sides, especially when it comes to religion. Some theologians who claim to be evangelicals argue that people can find true salvation through the other religions of the world, whether they believe in Jesus or not.[14] Not surprisingly, their students are starting to believe them. A survey conducted by James Davison Hunter of the University of Virginia revealed that a majority of students at Christian colleges and seminaries doubt whether faith in Jesus Christ is really necessary. They do not want to take sides.

When it comes to salvation, however, people have always had to take sides. They had to do it in the days of Joshua when the children of Israel were surrounded by foreign religions.

Joshua told them they had to take a stand: "'. . . choose for yourselves this day whom you will serve. . . .'" (Josh. 24:15).

The prophet Elijah gave people the same choice. "'How long will you waver between two opinions? If the LORD is God, follow him; but if Baal is God, follow him'" (1 Kings 18:21). It had to be one or the other. It could not be both, for that is not how truth operates. You cannot make up your own truth any more than you can make up your own multiplication tables. Anyone who wants to come to the true God must reject every false god.

Jesus Christ demands the same choice. If you want to be on the side of truth, you must take your stand with him. You must listen to him. You must believe in him. You must be true to him. If you are a follower of Jesus, then you stand for truth in the world. The people of God are people of the truth.

What it means to stand for the truth is to tell the truth *all the time*. In this age of moral relativism, most people only tell the truth when they think it matters. Even a liar tells the truth every now and then, when it suits his purposes.

What makes God's people different is that they are truth-tellers. A Christian "lives by the truth" (John 3:21). The truth always matters to believers, just because it is the truth. As John Piper writes, "Not to care about truth is not to care about God. To love God passionately is to love truth passionately."[15]

Sadly, most people do not give up lying altogether when they join the church; their lies just get more sophisticated. They give up the bold-faced lie, the premeditated prevarication, and the out-and-out falsehood. But soon they master the slight exaggeration, the misleading suggestion, and the damaging insinuation.

Before you know it, you become a real hypocrite, someone who pretends to be on God's side but really isn't. In order to keep up appearances, you tell the truth selectively. Propping up your reputation becomes a full-time job. You become your own spin doctor, always tweaking the truth to your advantage.

It is easy to see why hypocrisy is so offensive to God. It is the falsity he hates. He is the true God. Since he is the true God, he desires truth "in the inner parts" (Ps. 51:6), meaning truth at the very center of one's being. But the hypocrite's whole life is a lie. Therefore, hypocrites cannot be on the side of Christ. They are on the side of Satan, the father of lies (John 8:44), and they are destined to live with him forever in hell (Rev. 21:8). It is said of those who serve Satan: "They perish because they refused to love the truth and so be saved" (2 Thess. 2:10).

If you stand for Jesus, then you must stand for the truth. Be true to your friends. Speak as well of them in private as you do in public. Be true to your word. Keep your promises and honor your commitments. Be true to your family. Be open and honest with your spouse. Be on your guard against secret sins.

If you stand for Jesus, be true to your church. Keep the vows you have made to your congregation. Remember what happened to Ananias and Sapphira when they lied to the church about their offering (Acts 5:1-11)! "Each of you must put off falsehood and speak truthfully to his neighbor, for we are all members of one body" (Eph. 4:25).

As you put off falsehood, remember to speak "the truth in love" (4:15). There is too much flattery in the church and too much slander but too little compassionate candor. Thomas Boston, who had both compassion and candor, applied this verse to his congregation: "Let the strictest rules of truth and sincerity be observed by you in all your dealings and intercourse with men. Lay aside all lying, falsehood, and dissimulation, all equivocations and secret reservations in your words and promises, and speak the truth every man with his neighbor."[16]

If you stand for Jesus, be true in your business dealings. As the Puritan Thomas Watson warned, "He that will lie in his trade shall lie in hell."[17] Do not exaggerate on your résumé. Do not conceal a fraud. Do not misrepresent your product. Do not cheat on your clients or your taxes.

If you stand for Jesus, seek the truth in your studies. Do not cheat. Do not cut corners in your research. Make and perform works of art that display artistry rather than artifice.

If you stand for Jesus, hold on to the truth in your entertainment. The Bible says, "Whatever is true . . . think about such things" (Phil. 4:8). If we are to think about true things, then we ought to be reading, watching, and listening to true things.

Finally, be true to your faith. Remain true to the Lord Jesus Christ with all your heart. If you are his follower, then stand for nothing but the truth.

CHAPTER 13

THE GREATEST LOVE STORY
EVER TOLD

The Whole Story of Salvation

———— ⌾ ————

God is love. Whoever lives in love lives in God, and God in him.

1 JOHN 4:16B

God is love. That is the simplest definition of God there is.

Not "love is God," as if love were more important or more fundamental than the other divine attributes. This is the error of liberal theology in all its forms, to elevate God's love by denigrating his holiness. But the attributes of God cannot be separated. They cannot even be prioritized. The God who loves is the very same God who judges. His love is a holy, holy, holy love.

It is not even enough to say, "God loves." Love is more than a verb for God; he *is* love. It is his very being and nature. Whenever God loves, it is a revelation of his loving essence. Love is who God is.

It is hard to know how best to define God's love, or if such a definition should even be attempted. Somewhere John Calvin (1509-1564) wrote, "No figure of speech can describe God's extraordinary affection toward us, for it is infinite and various: so that, if all that can be said or imagined about love were brought together in one, yet it would be surpassed by the greatness of the love of God."

Perhaps we can say that God's love is his commitment to do good to all creatures and to give himself to his people through Jesus Christ. J. I. Packer offers a fuller definition: "God's love is an exercise of His goodness toward individual sinners whereby, having identified Himself with their welfare, He has given His Son to be their Saviour, and now brings them to know and enjoy Him in a covenant relation."[1]

As these definitions indicate, love is part of God's goodness. This probably explains why the Puritans who wrote the Westminster Shorter Catechism did not include love in their definition of God (although they did mention it elsewhere). The love of God is the supreme manifestation of divine goodness to sinners.

LOVE PURPOSED

God loves us more than we can ever say. But we can tell the story of his love. It is a story it takes the whole Bible to tell, the greatest love story ever told. In a way, it is the only love story there is. All the other love stories we tell are plagiarized from it. The reason we tell stories about romance (such as *Sleeping Beauty*) and rescue (such as *Robin Hood*) is ultimately because God loves us and saves us.

The story of God's love began long, long ago in the bright mystery of eternity past where love was *purposed*. Long before you were born, before the first Christmas, before the Great Flood, before the heavens were separated from the earth, even before the beginning of time itself, God planned his love for you.

God is love. His love is as permanent as the rest of his attributes. With that eternal love he has always loved you. "The LORD appeared to us in the past, saying: 'I have loved you with an everlasting love; I have drawn you with loving-kindness'" (Jer. 31:3). If you are God's child, then divine affection has rested upon you for as long as there has been a God—in other words, forever.

From all eternity, the Father, the Son, and the Holy Spirit took counsel together. They determined to make a universe that would be supremely expressive of their love. In that universe they would display a general benevolence for all their creatures.

But God, in his triune being, also decided to place his special affection upon a chosen people. This is the wondrous mystery described in the first chapter of Ephesians:

> *Praise be to the God and Father of our Lord Jesus Christ, who has blessed us in the heavenly realms with every spiritual blessing in Christ. For he chose us in him before the creation of the world to be holy and blameless in his sight. In love he predestined us to be adopted as his sons through Jesus Christ, in accordance with his pleasure and will—to the praise of his glorious grace, which he has freely given us in the One he loves.* (Eph. 1:3-6)

Notice where God's affections lie. He loves his Son, Jesus Christ, and he loves us (cf. John 17:23). Therefore, it is *in love* that he predestined us through Jesus Christ.

Some people have the mistaken idea that predestination is a dark and dangerous doctrine, as if there were some kind of hostility behind it. But the Bible connects divine predestination with divine affection. The choice of salvation comes from God's heart as well as from his will. It is always predestination *in love*, so that God's eternal choice expresses his eternal compassion.

The proper response to God's loving predestination can only be joy, never fear. "How blessed to know," writes A. W. Pink, "that the great and holy God loved His people before heaven and earth were called into existence, that He had set His heart upon them from all eternity."[2]

The fact that God's love was purposed from all eternity proves that salvation begins with God. Reformation theology is known for teaching the sovereignty of God's grace. Salvation is all of God and not of men. But Reformation theology also teaches the sovereignty of God's love. "We love because he first loved us" (1 John 4:19), and the divine "first" goes all the way back to eternity past.

God does not love us because we first loved him. If that were the case, then he would never love us! We are not adorable, in the sense that we are worthy of his adoration. We are neither lovely nor lovable. As Samuel Crossman (c. 1624-1683) wrote in one of his hymns:

> *My song is love unknown,*
> *My Savior's love to me,*
> *Love to the loveless shown,*
> *That they might lovely be.*

God would never come to us and say, "You know, I'm kind of attracted to you. Are you interested in maybe having some kind of relationship?"

On the contrary, a relationship with God flows out of his eternal, electing love. "Love among men is awakened by something in the beloved," writes J. I. Packer, "but the love of God is free, spontaneous, unevoked, uncaused."[3] Scripture thus teaches us to "know and rely on the love God has for us" (1 John 4:16a). His is the first and the best love. It is not a love that responds; it is a love that compels.

Why does God love? When Moses tried to explain it, he had to admit that there really is no explanation. "The LORD did not set his affection on you and choose you because you were more numerous than other peoples. . . . But it was because the LORD loved you . . . that he redeemed you from the land of slavery" (Deut. 7:7-8). In other words, God loves you because he loves you. How is that for an answer?

God does not love you because you have a lot to offer. He

loves you, as he has always loved you, because he is love. "He hath loved us, He hath loved us," wrote Charles Wesley (1707-1788). Why? "Because he would love."[4]

LOVE PROMISED

The love God purposed in eternity was *promised* in history. The Old Testament tells the true story of "the LORD's eternal love for Israel" (1 Kings 10:9). It is a love story that holds the promise of an even greater love to come.

God's unfailing love explains the great events of the Old Testament. In love God planted a garden in the East for Adam and Eve. When they sinned, it was in love that he gave them the promise of salvation. In love God shut the door of the ark to save Noah and his family from the Great Flood.

In love God established a covenant with Abraham, Isaac, and Jacob, promising to give them a land and a people. He gave them many great and precious promises because he loved them.

In love God delivered his people out of Egypt. "'When Israel was a child I loved him,'" said God, "'and out of Egypt I called my son'" (Hos. 11:1). In love he gave them his commandments and showed his favor to those who kept them. In love he defeated all their enemies and brought them into the Promised Land. In love he established a kingdom and promised David an eternal throne.

God graced his people with his loving presence, especially at the temple in Jerusalem. When they went there to worship, they sang about his unfailing love. "Give thanks to the LORD, for he is good; his love endures forever" (1 Chron. 16:34). This refrain is repeated throughout the songs of the Old Testament.

It was also in love that God allowed his temple to be destroyed and his people deported to Babylon. But even through their long exile, he kept the love covenant he had made with them. Through their suffering they learned to love him with all their hearts, until eventually, in love, he brought them back home to rebuild Jerusalem.

From beginning to end, the whole story is about God's love. The prophet Isaiah summarized the entire epic adventure in one sentence: "In his love and mercy he redeemed them; he lifted them up and carried them all the days of old" (Isa. 63:9). There is a similar summary at the end of Psalm 107. After recounting the saving acts of God in history, the psalmist writes, "Whoever is wise, let him heed these things and consider the great love of the LORD" (v. 43). The God of the Old Testament is a God abounding in love.

God's love also explains the images of the Old Testament. If you want to know what kind of love God promises, just look at the pictures. His love is like a scorching hot romance. "Let him kiss me with the kisses of his mouth—for your love is more delightful than wine" (Song 1:2). "My lover is mine and I am his" (2:16a). Then the romance becomes a marriage. God says, "I will betroth you to me forever; I will betroth you in righteousness and justice, in love and compassion" (Hos. 2:19).

The scene changes. The love of God is like a mother with her little child. She cradles her baby in her arms. Softly she sings a lullaby. In the same way, "the LORD your God . . . will take great delight in you, he will quiet you with his love, he will rejoice over you with singing" (Zeph. 3:17).

Or the love of God is like a father's love for his son. "As a father has compassion on his children, so the LORD has compassion on those who fear him" (Ps. 103:13). I remember riding home from church on an English double-decker bus with my firstborn son on my lap. I stroked his hair, caressed his smiling cheeks, and said, "This is *my* beloved son." That is what God's love for us is like—a father's compassion for his children.

These are the illustrations for the love story of salvation, the greatest love story ever told. The love of God is like a man and a woman who fall in love, get married, start a family, and love their children. The images of the Old Testament, like the events, hold the promise of love.

The promises of love centered on the coming Messiah, the one Isaiah wrote about, when he said, "In love a throne will be established; in faithfulness a man will sit on it—one from the house of David" (Isa. 16:5a). This is what God promised—a Messiah to come and rule from the throne of his love.

LOVE PERSONIFIED

Then one day the promise was fulfilled. The love purposed in eternity and promised in history was *personified* in the Nativity. What the carols say is true: Love came down at Christmas. "This is how God showed his love among us: He sent his one and only Son into the world that we might live through him" (1 John 4:9). God sent us his love by sending us his Son.

Consider what the coming of the Son tells us about the love of the Father. The great Swiss theologian Francis Turretin (1623-1687) once tried to explain the wonders of God's love. He wrote, "These [three] things in the highest manner commend the love of God toward us: (1) the majesty of the lover; (2) the poverty and unworthiness of the loved; (3) the worth of him in whom we are loved."[5]

These three things are true about God's love for us in Christ. First, *our lover is majestic.* We are loved by the Almighty God who rules the universe from his exalted throne. God's love is great because he is worthy.

Second, *we are poor and unworthy.* We are so lost and miserable in our sins that we have nothing to offer to God. Yet God loves us in spite of ourselves. God's love is great because we are unworthy.

The third thing has to do with the way we are loved. *We are loved by God in Jesus Christ.* His worthiness proves the value of God's love. Turretin explains it like this: "He in whom they are beloved is Christ, the delight of his heavenly Father and the 'express image of his person,' than whom he could have given nothing more excellent, nothing dearer, even if he had given the whole universe."[6]

God has shown us his great love by giving us his greatest gift. God the Father loves God the Son (John 3:35; 5:20). The Son is the apple of his fatherly eye. When Jesus was baptized, for example, the voice from heaven said, "'This is my Son, whom I love; with him I am well pleased'" (Matt. 3:17).

What does it tell us, then, that God has given us his own beloved Son? It tells us, in a way nothing else could, that God loves us. "God so loved the world that he gave his one and only Son, that whoever believes in him shall not perish but have eternal life" (John 3:16). J. I. Packer writes, "The measure of love is how much it gives, and the measure of the love of God is the gift of His only Son to be made man, and to die for sins, and so to become the one mediator who can bring us to God."[7] In sending us his Son, the Father sent us his love.

The Son of God is love personified. In the words of "Silent Night," he is "Son of God, love's pure light." If God is love, and if Jesus is God, then Jesus is love. He is love incarnate. He is the perfect expression of divine love, as he is the perfect expression of every divine attribute.

There is divine love in the teaching of Jesus, who said, "'Love the Lord your God with all your heart and with all your soul and with all your mind. . . . Love your neighbor as yourself'" (Matt. 22:37, 39).

There is divine love in the miracles of Jesus. We see it in the way he fed the hungry, gave sight to the blind, and made the lame to walk. We see it in his healing touch to cure disease and in his living breath to raise the dead.

There is divine love in the forgiveness of Jesus. He forgave sinners and tax collectors. He forgave women who practiced adultery. He even forgave his enemies.

There is divine love in the tears of Jesus. He shed tears at the death of his friend Lazarus, grieving for the pain and sorrow death brings into the world. He wept over Jerusalem, grieving for the lost and sorry condition of humanity.

In his words and deeds, in his joys and sorrows, Jesus Christ is love personified.

LOVE POURED OUT

Then one day Jesus took his love and poured it all out. The love purposed from all eternity was *poured out* in agony on the cross. Jesus did many loving things during his life, but the most loving thing of all was what he did in his death.

The crucifixion is the climactic chapter in the greatest love story ever told. As John begins to tell about it in his Gospel, he explains that "Jesus knew that the time had come for him to leave this world and go to the Father. Having loved his own who were in the world, he now showed them the full extent of his love" (John 13:1). This is a Scripture phrase to be savored—"the full extent of his love." Jesus had always loved his disciples, but now he would show them the height, the length, the width, and the depth of his love.

When John spoke about the full extent of Christ's love, he was talking about his sufferings and death. There were certain endearments of divine affection that had not yet been revealed in all their tenderness. In order for us to know the full extent of God's love, it was necessary for Jesus to suffer and to die for our sins.

There was love in the Garden of Gethsemane, love in the kissing betrayal. There was love in the Praetorium of Pilate, love in the thorny crown. There was love on the hill of Calvary, love on the wooden cross. Why else did Jesus suffer these things, if not because he loves us?

The cross reveals the heart of God. In the cross we know

that God loves us in spite of our rebellion. In the cross we know that he forgives our sins. In the cross we know that he loves us all the way.

At the same time, the cross reveals the heart of Jesus Christ. Sacrifice is the best proof of love. Anyone who is truly in love will make bold sacrifices for the beloved. And the ultimate sacrifice, of course, is death. Therefore, a sacrifice unto death is the ultimate proof of supreme love. "'Greater love has no one than this,'" said Jesus, "'that he lay down his life for his friends'" (John 15:13).

That is exactly what Jesus proceeded to do. "Very rarely will anyone die for a righteous man, though for a good man someone might possibly dare to die. But God demonstrates his own love for us in this: While we were still sinners, Christ died for us" (Rom. 5:7-8).

Is it any wonder that when the writers of the New Testament looked back to the cross, what they saw there was this divine attribute of love poured out in overflowing abundance?

Live a life of love, just as Christ loved us and gave himself up for us as a fragrant offering and sacrifice to God. (Eph. 5:2)

This is how we know what love is: Jesus Christ laid down his life for us. (1 John 3:16)

This is love: not that we loved God, but that he loved us and sent his Son as an atoning sacrifice for our sins. (1 John 4:10)

To him who loves us and has freed us from our sins by his blood, and has made us to be a kingdom and priests to serve his God and Father—to him be glory and power for ever and ever! Amen. (Rev. 1:5b-6)

If you want to receive God's love, you must go to the cross. That is the place to obtain his love because that is where God poured it out. If you want God to save you from sin and death, you must go to the cross where Christ died for your sins.

The love God demonstrated on the cross must be received personally. To put it another way, the greatest love story ever told must become your own life story. You must believe that Jesus died for your own sins. We learn this from Scripture, which teaches us to say, "I live by faith in the Son of God, who loved me and gave himself for me" (Gal. 2:20b).

We also learn this from other Christians. One example is Charles Wesley, the great English hymn writer. Wesley had always heard that Jesus Christ had died on the cross for sins. But he did not become a true Christian until he was convinced of his personal need for a Savior. In the same year he finally trusted Christ for his salvation, he wrote:

> *And can it be that I should gain*
> *An int'rest in the Savior's blood?*
> *Died he for me, who caused his pain?*
> *For me, who him to death pursued?*
> *Amazing love! How can it be*
> *That thou, my God, shouldst die for me?*

Wesley had received God's love personally through the death of Christ on the cross.

LOVE PERFECTED

The death of Christ on the cross is the most poignant chapter in the greatest love story ever told. But how does the story end? Is it "happily ever after"?

Indeed it is. Someday God's love will be *perfected*. The same love that was purposed from eternity, promised in history, personified in the Nativity, and poured out in agony will be perfected in glory. The Bible says that "love never fails" (1 Cor. 13:8a). The reason it never fails is because God never fails.

This means that the greatest love story ever told will never come to an end. There is nothing, absolutely nothing, that can stop God's love. "For I am convinced that neither death nor life, neither angels nor demons, neither the present nor the future, nor any powers, neither height nor depth, nor anything else in all creation, will be able to separate us from the love of God that is in Christ Jesus our Lord" (Rom. 8:38-39).

Nothing can separate you from God's love in Christ. He will keep loving you, and loving you, and loving you until you are full of his love. By the time God has loved you all the way through, you will "have power, together with all the saints, to grasp how wide and long and high and deep is the love of Christ, and to know this love that surpasses knowledge—that you may be filled to the measure of all the fullness of God" (Eph. 3:17b-19).

If you know Jesus Christ, that is starting to happen already. The same love that was poured out for you by God's Son is being poured into you by God's Spirit. "God has poured out his love into our hearts by the Holy Spirit, whom he has given us" (Rom. 5:5). Literally, God is "flooding" your heart with his love. He is giving you an abundant love to love others deeply, from the heart, and to adore God himself.

Perhaps you do not love very much, but if you know God at all, then you must love at least a little. The Bible teaches that "whoever does not love does not know God, because God is love" (1 John 4:8). So you must love a little, but possibly not very much. Certainly not as much as God loves you.

Realize that you will never learn how to love God or anyone else out of your own heart. The love cannot come from you; it has to come from God. "Everyone who loves has been born of God and knows God" (1 John 4:7b). Those who love most and love best are those who have opened their hearts to receive the love of God.

If you are not much of a lover, the English poet William

Cowper has written a prayer for you. Cowper's prayer is suitable for anyone who wants to learn to love, and especially to love the God who is "infinite, eternal, and unchangeable in his being, wisdom, power, holiness, justice, goodness, and truth":

> *Lord, it is my chief complaint,*
> *That my love is weak and faint;*
> *Yet I love thee and adore.*
> *Oh, for grace to love thee more!*

In response to this prayer, God gives "grace to all who love our Lord Jesus Christ with an undying love" (Eph. 6:24).

AFTERWORD

The Scottish theologian Thomas Boston once wrote a treatise, "Of God and His Perfections." As he came to the end of his work, Boston was conscious of how much more could be written about God and how much more could be learned. He wrote:

> Thus we have given you a short description of what God is. Imperfect it is, and imperfect it must be, seeing he is incomprehensible. Do ye study to believe what is taught you of God, and apply to him, through the Son of his love, for further discoveries of his glorious perfections and excellencies; and at length ye shall see him as he is, having a more enlarged and extensive knowledge of him, his nature and ways; though even then ye will not be able to comprehend him. For it was a wise and judicious answer of one that was asked, What God is? that if he knew that fully, he should be a God himself. And indeed that being which we can comprehend, cannot be God, because he is infinite. O study God and ye will increase in the knowledge of him.[1]

We are not finished learning the attributes of God. We have only just begun. Because God is infinite in his perfections, there is always more of him to know. To God alone be all the praise!

NOTES

Preface

1 Charles Haddon Spurgeon, *The New Park Street Pulpit* (1855; repr. Pasadena, TX: Pilgrim, 1975), 1:1.

2 Philipp Melanchthon, introduction to *Loci Communes* (1st ed.), in Christian History Institute's *Glimpses*, no. 98 (1998), 4.

3 Martin Luther, in Paul Althaus, *The Theology of Martin Luther* (Philadelphia: Fortress, 1966), 16.

Chapter 1: To God Be the Glory

1 David F. Wells, *God in the Wasteland: The Reality of Truth in a World of Fading Dreams* (Grand Rapids, MI: Eerdmans, 1994), 88.

2 Thomas Watson, *A Body of Divinity*, rev. ed. (London, 1692; repr. Edinburgh: Banner of Truth, 1965), 6.

Chapter 2: God Is Spirit

1 See William Barker, *Puritan Profiles* (Fearn, Ross-shire: Christian Focus, 1996), 110.

2 James Benjamin Green, *A Harmony of the Westminster Presbyterian Standards, with Explanatory Notes* (Philadelphia: John Knox, 1951), 26.

3 Craig A. Evans, "Crisis in the Middle East," *Christian History*, 59 (vol. 17, no. 3), 20-23 (p. 21).

4 Ibid.

5 R. V. G. Tasker, *The Gospel According to St. John: An Introduction and Commentary*, Tyndale New Testament Commentaries (Grand Rapids, MI: Eerdmans, 1960), 75.

6 See John Macdonald, *The Theology of the Samaritans* (Philadelphia: Westminster Press, 1964), 327-33.

7 Quoted in H. L. Strack and P. Billerbeck, *Kommentar zum Neuen Testament aus Talmud und Midrasch*, 4 vols. (Munich: Beck'sche Verlagsbuchhandlung, 1922-28), 1:549.

8 Andrew Murray, *With Christ in the School of Prayer* (Westwood, NJ: Revell, 1953), 22-23.

9 James Montgomery Boice, *The Gospel of John: An Expositional Commentary* (Grand Rapids, MI: Zondervan, 1985), 253.

10 Philipp Melanchthon, in Thomas Watson, *A Body of Divinity*, rev. ed. (London, 1692; repr. Edinburgh: Banner of Truth, 1965), 50.

Chapter 3: God Is Everywhere

1 Debby Anderson, *God Is with Me*, 4th ed. (Cincinnati, OH: Standard Publishing, 1995).

2 Thomas Watson, *A Body of Divinity*, rev. ed. (London, 1692; repr. Edinburgh: Banner of Truth, 1965), 54.

3 A. W. Tozer, *The Attributes of God: A Journey into the Father's Heart* (Camp Hill, PA: Christian Publications, 1997), 119-20.

4 John Wesley, "God's Omnipresence," in *Classic Sermons on the Attributes of God*, ed. Warren W. Wiersbe (Grand Rapids, MI: Kregel, 1989), 111-18 (p. 113).

5 Ray Bakke, *A Theology as Big as the City* (Downers Grove, IL: InterVarsity, 1997), 98.

6 Donald Grey Barnhouse, in James Montgomery Boice, *The Minor Prophets* (Grand Rapids, MI: Kregel, 1996), 216.

7 Joyce Baldwin, *Jonah*, in *The Minor Prophets: An Exegetical and Expository Commentary*, ed. Thomas Edward McComiskey, 2 vols. (Grand Rapids, MI: Baker, 1993), 2:543-90 (p. 553).

8 William Jefferson Clinton, in "The Starr Report," *Philadelphia Inquirer*, September 13, 1998, S4.

9 Brother Lawrence, *The Practice of the Presence of God* (Old Tappan, NJ: Fleming Revell, 1958), 45.

10 Boice, *Minor Prophets*, 227-28.

11 Francis Thompson, "The Hound of Heaven," in *The Oxford Book of Christian Verse*, ed. Lord David Cecil (Oxford: Oxford University Press, 1940), 510-15.

12 Bakke, *Theology as Big*, 98.

13 Stephen Charnock, *The Existence and Attributes of God* (Ann Arbor, MI: Banner of Truth, 1958), 177.

Chapter 4: Now to the King Eternal

1 Arthur W. Pink, *The Attributes of God* (Grand Rapids, MI: Baker, 1961), 5.

2 Thomas Boston, *The Complete Works of the Late Rev. Thomas Boston of Ettrick*, ed. Samuel M'Millan, 12 vols. (London, 1853; repr. Wheaton, IL: Richard Owen Roberts, 1980), 1:83.

3 Augustine, in Stephen Charnock, *The Existence and Attributes of God* (Ann Arbor, MI: Banner of Truth, 1958), 72.

4 Herman Bavinck, *The Doctrine of God*, trans. William Hendricksen (Edinburgh: Banner of Truth, 1977), 156.

5 Mihaly Csikszentmihalyi, *Flow: The Psychology of Optimal Experience* (New York: HarperCollins, 1991).

6 C. S. Lewis, in A. W. Tozer, *The Attributes of God: A Journey into the Father's Heart* (Camp Hill, PA: Christian Publications, 1997), 5-6.

7 *International Bible Dictionary* (Plainfield, NJ: Logos International, 1977), 49.

8 Thomas Watson, *A Body of Divinity*, rev. ed. (London, 1692; repr. Edinburgh: Banner of Truth, 1965), 63.

Chapter 5: God Does Not Change

1 Arthur W. Pink, *The Attributes of God* (Grand Rapids, MI: Baker, 1961), 32.

2 James Montgomery Boice, *Foundations of the Christian Faith*, rev. ed. (Downers Grove, IL: InterVarsity, 1986), 141.

3 Arthur John Gossip, "Immutability: God's Crowning Attribute," in *Classic Sermons on the Attributes of God*, ed. Warren W. Wiersbe (Grand Rapids, MI: Kregel, 1989), 146-58 (pp. 150-51).

4 Stephen Charnock, *The Existence and Attributes of God* (Ann Arbor, MI: Banner of Truth, 1958), 79.

5 Thomas Boston, *The Complete Works of the Late Rev. Thomas Boston of Ettrick*, ed. Samuel M'Millan, 12 vols. (London, 1853; repr. Wheaton, IL: Richard Owen Roberts, 1980), 1:83.

6 See Clark Pinnock, et al., *The Openness of God: A Biblical Challenge to the Traditional Understanding of God* (Downers Grove, IL: InterVarsity, 1994).

7 Thomas Watson, *A Body of Divinity*, rev. ed. (London, 1692; repr. Edinburgh: Banner of Truth, 1965), 69.

8 R. Laird Harris, ed., *Theological Wordbook of the Old Testament* (Chicago: Moody, 1980), 2:571.

9 J. I. Packer, *Knowing God* (Downers Grove, IL: InterVarsity, 1973), 72.

10 A. W. Tozer, *The Knowledge of the Holy* (New York: Harper & Row, 1961), 59.

11 Pink, *Attributes of God*, 34.

12 Oliver Cromwell, in Gossip, "Immutability," in *Classic Sermons*, 157.

Chapter 6: The Great I AM

1 W. H. Auden, in Darryl Tippens, Stephen Weathers, and Jack Welch, eds., *Shadow and Light: Literature and the Life of Truth* (Abilene, TX: ACU Press, 1997), 357.

2 Thomas Altizer, in William E. Hordern, *A Layman's Guide to Protestant Theology,* rev. ed. (New York: Macmillan, 1968), 239.

3 *Westminster Confession of Faith,* II.2, referring to Romans 11:36.

4 See Hugh Ross, *The Creator and the Cosmos: How the Greatest Scientific Discoveries of the Century Reveal God* (Colorado Springs, CO: NavPress, 1993), 105-14.

5 Paul Davies, *The Cosmic Blueprint* (New York: Simon & Schuster, 1988), 203.

6 Richard Dawkins, *The Blind Watchmaker: Why the Evidence of Evolution Reveals a Universe Without Design* (New York: Norton, 1996), 21.

7 Francis Crick, *What Mad Pursuit,* in William A. Dembski, "Science and Design," *First Things,* 86 (October, 1998), 21-27 (p. 21).

8 See William Dembski, *The Design Inference* (Cambridge: Cambridge University Press, 1998).

9 Francis Turretin, *Institutes of Elenctic Theology,* trans. George Musgrave Giger, ed. James T. Dennison, Jr., 3 vols. (Phillipsburg, NJ: Presbyterian & Reformed, 1992-1997), III.i.3, 1:169.

10 Herman Bavinck, *The Doctrine of God,* trans. William Hendricksen (Edinburgh: Banner of Truth, 1977), 85.

11 Matthew Henry, *Commentary on the Whole Bible,* 6 vols. (New York: Fleming H. Revell, n.d.), 1:284.

12 J. I. Packer, *Knowing God* (Downers Grove, IL: InterVarsity, 1973), 69.

13 *Westminster Confession of Faith,* II.2.

Chapter 7: God Has All the Answers

1 Arthur W. Pink, *The Attributes of God* (Grand Rapids, MI: Baker, 1961), 13.

2 Herman Bavinck, *The Doctrine of God,* trans. William Hendricksen (Edinburgh: Banner of Truth, 1977), 195.

3 Sinclair B. Ferguson, *A Heart for God* (Edinburgh: Banner of Truth, 1987), 71.

4 Anselm, in A. W. Tozer, *The Attributes of God: A Journey into the Father's Heart* (Camp Hill, PA: Christian Publications, 1997), 63.

5 Thomas Boston, *The Complete Works of the Late Rev. Thomas Boston of Ettrick,* ed. Samuel M'Millan, 12 vols. (London, 1853; repr. Wheaton, IL: Richard Owen Roberts, 1980), 1:86-7.

6 Dan G. McCartney, *Why Does It Have to Hurt? The Meaning of Christian Suffering* (Phillipsburg, NJ: Presbyterian & Reformed, 1998), 40.

7 C. S. Lewis, *God in the Dock: Essays on Theology and Ethics,* ed. Walter Hooper (Grand Rapids, MI: Eerdmans, 1970), 244.

8 Eugene H. Peterson, *Run with the Horses: The Quest for Life at Its Best* (Downers Grove, IL: InterVarsity, 1983), 37-38.

9 J. I. Packer, *Knowing God* (Downers Grove, IL: InterVarsity, 1973), 96.

10 Boston, *Complete Works,* 1:89.

Chapter 8: The Lord God Omnipotent Reigns

1 Charles Hartshorne, *Omnipotence and Other Theological Mistakes* (Albany, NY: State University of New York Press, 1984).

2 Stephen Charnock, *The Existence and Attributes of God* (Ann Arbor, MI: Banner of Truth, 1958), 364.

3 R. V. G. Tasker, *The Gospel According to St. John,* Tyndale New Testament Commentaries (Leicester: InterVarsity, 1960), 138.

4 John Daniel Jones, "The Sovereignty of God," in *Classic Sermons on the Attributes of God,* ed. Warren W. Wiersbe (Grand Rapids, MI: Kregel, 1989), 41-55 (p. 53).

5 C. John Miller, *Powerful Evangelism for the Powerless,* rev. ed. (Phillipsburg, NJ: Presbyterian & Reformed, 1997), 4.

6 Ibid., 4.
7 Charnock, *Existence and Attributes of God*, 438.

Chapter 9: Holy, Holy, Holy

1 James Montgomery Boice, *Foundations of the Christian Faith*, rev. ed. (Downers Grove, IL: InterVarsity, 1986), 125.
2 J. A. Motyer, *The Prophecy of Isaiah* (Downers Grove, IL: InterVarsity, 1993), 77.
3 Ibid., 75.
4 Boice, *Foundations*, 133.
5 A. W. Tozer, *The Attributes of God: A Journey into the Father's Heart* (Camp Hill, PA: Christian Publications, 1997), 172.

Chapter 10: The Justice of It All

1 William Shakespeare, *The Tragedy of Othello, the Moor of Venice*, ed. Alvin Kernan (New York: New American Library, 1963), act 4, scene 1.
2 Arthur W. Pink, *The Attributes of God* (Grand Rapids, MI: Baker, 1961), 76.
3 Paul Cook, "Preaching and the Wrath of God," *Banner of Truth*, 411 (December 1997), 10-17 (p. 12).
4 Pink, *Attributes of God*, 75.
5 J. I. Packer, *Knowing God* (Downers Grove, IL: InterVarsity, 1973), 139.
6 Augustine, in Thomas Watson, *A Body of Divinity*, rev. ed. (London, 1692; repr. Edinburgh: Banner of Truth, 1965), 90.
7 Jonathan Edwards, "The Manner of Seeking Salvation," in *The Works of Jonathan Edwards*, 2 vols. (1834; repr. Edinburgh: Banner of Truth, 1974), 2:51-57 (p. 54).
8 Thomas Boston, *The Complete Works of the Late Rev. Thomas Boston of Ettrick*, ed. Samuel M'Millan, 12 vols. (London, 1853; repr. Wheaton, IL: Richard Owen Roberts, 1980), 1:109.
9 Pink, *Attributes of God*, 78.
10 Packer, *Knowing God*, 127.
11 Ibid., 133.

Chapter 11: God Is Good . . . All the Time

1 C. S. Lewis, *The Lion, the Witch and the Wardrobe* (London: Collins, 1974), 77.
2 Thomas Manton, in Arthur W. Pink, *The Attributes of God* (Grand Rapids, MI: Baker, 1961), 52.
3 Herman Bavinck, *Systematic Theology*, 4th ed. (Grand Rapids, MI: Eerdmans, 1941), 70.
4 Herman Bavinck, *The Doctrine of God*, trans. William Hendricksen (Edinburgh: Banner of Truth, 1977), 204.
5 J. I. Packer, *Knowing God* (Downers Grove, IL: InterVarsity, 1973), 147.
6 Stephen Charnock, *The Existence and Attributes of God* (Ann Arbor, MI: Banner of Truth, 1958), 533-657.
7 Charles Spurgeon, in Arthur W. Pink, *The Attributes of God* (Grand Rapids, MI: Baker, 1961), 55.
8 Phillip Keller, *A Shepherd Looks at Psalm 23* (Grand Rapids, MI: Zondervan, 1970), 35.
9 Ibid., 60.
10 *Philadelphia Inquirer*, November 25, 1998, A12.
11 F. W. Boreham, *In Pastures Green: A Ramble through the Twenty-third Psalm* (London: Epworth, 1954), 22-23.
12 F. B. Meyer, *The Shepherd Psalm* (Fort Washington, PA: Christian Literature Crusade, 1980), 52-53.
13 Boreham, *In Pastures Green*, 9.
14 James K. Wallace, "The Basque Sheepherder and the Shepherd Psalm," *Reader's Digest*, (July 1960).

15 Meyer, *Shepherd Psalm*, 110-111.
16 Terry L. Johnson, "The Pastor's Public Ministry," *Westminster Theological Journal*, vol. 60, no. 1 (Spring 1998), 131-152 (p. 150).

Chapter 12: Nothing but the Truth

1 Václav Havel, cited in a prospectus from the Komensky Institute of Prague.
2 Alistair Begg, *What Angels Wish They Knew* (Chicago: Moody Press, 1998).
3 Richard Stengel, "Lies My Presidents Told Me," *Time*, (August 31), 1998, 48-49.
4 Donald Rumsfeld, "Surprise, Surprise," *National Review*, (December 7), 1998, 51.
5 Daniel A. Farber and Suzanna Sherry, *Beyond All Reason: The Radical Assault on Truth in American Law* (New York: Oxford University Press, 1997).
6 See, for example, Sarah Coakley, *Christ Without Absolutes: A Study of the Christology of Ernst Troeltsch* (New York: Oxford University Press, 1989).
7 Ethicist Robert C. Solomon of the University of Texas, in Stengel, "Lies My Presidents Told Me," *Time*, 48. For an interesting analysis of deceit, see Diane M. Komp, *Anatomy of a Lie: The Truth About Lies and Why Good People Tell Them* (Grand Rapids, MI: Zondervan, 1998).
8 Thomas Harvey, "Truth May Soon Be More of a Stranger than Fiction," *Mission: America* (Summer 1998), 5-6.
9 Francis Bacon, "Of Truth," *Essays or Counsels—Civil and Moral*, Harvard Classics, 3 (New York: Collier, 1909), 7.
10 J. I. Packer, *Knowing God* (Downers Grove, IL: InterVarsity, 1973), 102.
11 Herman Bavinck, *The Doctrine of God*, trans. William Hendricksen (Edinburgh: Banner of Truth, 1977), 202.
12 H. R. Rookmaaker, *Modern Art and the Death of a Culture* (Wheaton, IL: Crossway, 1994), 234.
13 Ulrich Zwingli, in W. P. Stephens, *Zwingli: An Introduction to His Thought* (Oxford: Oxford University Press, 1992), 70.
14 A notorious example is Clark Pinnock's book *A Wideness in God's Mercy: The Finality of Jesus Christ in a World of Religions* (Grand Rapids, MI: Zondervan, 1992).
15 John Piper, *A Godward Life* (Sisters, OR: Multnomah, 1997), 106.
16 Thomas Boston, *The Complete Works of the Late Rev. Thomas Boston of Ettrick*, ed. Samuel M'Millan, 12 vols. (London, 1853; repr. Wheaton, IL: Richard Owen Roberts, 1980), 1:130.
17 Thomas Watson, *A Body of Divinity*, rev. ed. (London, 1692; repr. Edinburgh: Banner of Truth, 1965), 102.

Chapter 13: The Greatest Love Story Ever Told

1 J. I. Packer, *Knowing God* (Downers Grove, IL: InterVarsity, 1973), 111.
2 Arthur W. Pink, *The Attributes of God* (Grand Rapids, MI: Baker, 1961), 71.
3 Packer, *Knowing God*, 112.
4 Charles Wesley, in ibid.
5 Francis Turretin, *Institutes of Elenctic Theology*, trans. George Musgrave Giger, ed. James T. Dennison, Jr., 3 vols. (Phillipsburg, NJ: Presbyterian & Reformed, 1992-1997), III.xx.6 (1:242).
6 Ibid.
7 Packer, *Knowing God*, 114.

Afterword

1 Thomas Boston, *The Complete Works of the Late Rev. Thomas Boston of Ettrick*, ed. Samuel M'Millan, 12 vols. (London, 1853; repr. Wheaton, IL: Richard Owen Roberts, 1980), 1:130.

INDEX

SCRIPTURE INDEX